ROOTS & BRANCHES

A Legacy of Multicultural Music for Children

UNIVERSITY *of* LIMERICK

ROOTS & BRANCHES

A Legacy of Multicultural Music for Children

Patricia Shehan Campbell

Ellen McCullough-Brabson

Judith Cook Tucker

World Music Press

Roots & Branches:
A *Legacy of Multicultural Music for Children*

Compiled, transcribed and annotated by
Patricia Shehan Campbell
Ellen McCullough-Brabson
Judith Cook Tucker

Published by:

World Music Press
Judith Cook Tucker, Publisher; Editor-in-Chief
Claudia Chapman, Art Director, Assistant Editor
PO Box 2565 Danbury CT 06813-2565 (203) 748-1131

Acknowledgments
In addition to all who shared their musical memories for this collection,
the publisher wishes to thank the following:
• Claudia Chapman, editorial, art and design, networking, moral support, shared vision, finding and interviewing Gerard Leonard
and creating the section on Ireland and enriching England as well as several contributions throughout.
• Andrea Hanneman for expert knowledge and a summary of Russian history and culture.
• Ann Boocheever for activating the Russian network in record time and facilitating our link to Katya and her songs.
• Gary Louie, Sound Engineer, University of Washington and
• Kevin Campbell, Sound Engineer, University of New Mexico
• Glenn and Daniel Tucker, Joe and Bran Chapman for unwavering support and enthusiasm as we all slogged to the finish line.

ISBN 0-937203-55-6 Book/audio CD Set

Book and cover designed and typeset by Claudia Chapman
using a Macintosh Quadra 610 and Ready, Set, Go!® page layout software
Music typeset by Don Wallace and Judith Cook Tucker using MusicProse® and Finale®

Printed in the United States of America in accordance with all NAFTA regulations.
First printing May 1994.
6 7 8 9 10

Library of Congress Card Catalog Information
Roots & branches : a legacy of multicultural music for children/
[compiled, transcribed, and annotated by] Patricia Shehan Campbell,
Ellen McCullough-Brabson, Judith Cook Tucker. -- Original pbk. ed.
p. of music.
Unacc. melodies.
Includes bibliographical references (p.).
ISBN 0-937203-52-1 (pbk + cass.)
ISBN 0-937203-55-6 (pbk + CD)
1. Children's songs. I. Campbell, Patricia Shehan.
II. McCullough-Brabson, Ellen. III. Tucker, Judith Cook, 1947-
IV. Title: Roots and branches.
M1992.R76 1994   94-39274

About the Authors

Patricia Shehan Campbell, Ph. D.

Patricia Shehan Campbell is Professor of Music at the University of Washington. Her interest in world music has taken her as lecturer and researcher to Bulgaria, Hungary, China, Japan, Korea, Thailand, India and Australia. She is a consultant on music in early and middle childhood, world music education, and Dalcroze (eurhythmics, improvisation, and solfege). She is author of numerous publications that blend ethnomusicological and educational issues, including *Lessons from the World*, *Music in Childhood*, *Sounds of the World*: "Music of Eastern Europe," and "Music of Southeast Asia." She co-authored *From Rice Paddies and Temple Yards: Traditional Music of Vietnam*; *Silent Temples, Songful Hearts: Traditional Music of Cambodia*; *The Lion's Roar: Chinese Luogu Percussion Ensembles*; and *Multicultural Perspectives in Music Education*. She is chair of the Society for Ethnomusicology's Education Committee, and board member of the International Society for Music Education, The College Music Society, and the Journal of Research in Music Education. She is also an active member of the American Orff-Schulwerk Association and the Organization of American Kodaly Educators.

Ellen McCullough-Brabson, DMA

Ellen McCullough-Brabson is Professor of Music Education at the University of New Mexico. She received her Bachelor of Music degree from the Cincinnati Conservatory of Music and MM and DMA degrees from the University of Arizona. She has taken postdoctoral courses in ethnomusicology at the University of Washington where she studied Yoruba drumming and Indonesian gamelan. She has taught elementary general music in the Cincinnati, Tucson Sunnyside and Albuquerque Public School Districts. She is an active workshop clinician and has presented sessions on multicultural music for the International Society for Music Education, the Music Educators National Conference, the American Orff-Schulwerk National Conference, and numerous state and local teacher in-service days. she has taught summer multicultural music education workshops at several universities. Her published articles are on topics including world musics, Appalachian music, the dulcimer, and musical instruments from around the world. She was a contributing author to the MENC publications *Writings in Early Childhood* ("Early Childhood Multicultural Music Education") and *Multicultural Perspectives in Music Education* ("Music of the Southern Appalachian Mountains"). She narrates children's concerts for the Chamber Orchestra of Albuquerque and teaches Elderhostel courses. She experiences music daily with her daughter Jessie, age 6, and her son Rex, age 5.

Judith Cook Tucker

Judith Cook Tucker is publisher and editor-in-chief of World Music Press, which she founded in 1985 in response to the need for authentic, in-depth yet accessible multicultural materials for educators. She received a BA in Journalism and Anthropology from New York University and a Master of Arts in Liberal Studies from Wesleyan University (CT) with a concentration in ethnomusicology and music education. She is the co-author, with Abraham Kobina Adzenyah and Dumisani Maraire, of *Let Your Voice Be Heard! Songs from Ghana and Zimbabwe*, a contributing editor to *Music K-8 Magazine* and contributor to *MultiCultural Review*, and the editor of several book-and-tape sets of multicultural music including *La-Li-Luo Dance-Songs of the Chuxiong Yi*; *From Rice Paddies and Temple Yards: Traditional Music of Vietnam*; *Silent Temples, Songful Hearts: Traditional Music of Cambodia*; *A Singing Wind: Five Melodies from Ecuador*; *Pandemonium Rules: Steel Band Ensembles for Orff Instruments*; *The Lion's Roar: Chinese Luogu Percussion Ensembles* and *Moving Within the Circle: Contemporary Native American Music and Dance*. She regularly serves as a clinician at music education conferences and in-service workshops, as well as with choral groups performing pieces she has composed, arranged or published.

To Charlie and Andrew, and to my own people who have come before
and will follow me. —PSC

Special thanks and joyous singing to my family—John, Jessica and Rex,
to my friends, and to merry music-makers everywhere.—EMB

To the voices of the generations whispering in these pages—
you have not been, and will not be, forgotten.—JCT

❧Contents

List of Transcriptions

Preface

Singing is a human phenomenon that knows no cultural boundaries. Children begin singing even before they talk, musically babbling the sounds they hear at home. As their vocabulary grows, they play with words, rhythms and pitches, and gradually begin to express themselves in musically coherent ways through traditional songs and rhymes. In many cultures, children's songs function as a kind of shorthand, in which snippets of the core material of the culture are encapsulated. Children's songs help them to learn about themselves, about relationships and interactions with family members and friends, about how to play and work cooperatively, and about how to communicate appropriately. Children's songs even provide history, math, spelling and dance lessons! Deeply imbedded in the folklore of any group of people are their attitudes toward life itself. Just as many of the stories we tell to children have a moral or lesson to be learned, many of the songs we transmit also offer windows to the world we wish them to know. In this collection for example, "Zui, Zui Zukkorobashi" reveals a great deal concerning the traditional Japanese practice of taking the harvested tea leaves to the provincial lord each autumn, of children's impatience with the extended rituals of the passing procession, and of the play in which they engage themselves while adults bow humbly to the ambassadors. "Dahee Maatyaahr" is more than a description of one of Krishna's escapades; it reveals the tolerance of Indian parents for a bit of mischief among their little boys. "Tepok Amai-amai" describes children as ladybugs, grasshoppers and butterflies, and in doing so communicates the reality of the varied ethnic groups living in Malaysia, and the apparent acceptance of this diversity through affectionate names.

There are further ways songs intended for children's ears have implanted in them the values and philosophies of a society. It follows naturally, that in the nursery, preschool, kindergarten and primary grades an understanding of the meaning of cultural pluralism can be brought forth simply and effectively through the songs children sing. As young people seek broader knowledge, they find the world outside the home and school is even richer with exposure to diverse cultural expressions. Radio, television, and movies open their ears to a tasty sonic soup, filled with the wonderful nuances of each musical recipe the performers "cook" with.

This is an era of cultural pluralism, particularly in the United States, Canada, Australia and throughout the United Kingdom, and there are many musical tongues and cultural expressions found within geographic and socio-political borders. However, children continue to learn the lullabies, chants, and singing games of their parents' preference and heritage in the home, so that their first mother tongue music is that given them by their mothers, fathers, and siblings. Experiences in singing the songs of a variety of peoples of the world can open their ears and minds at an early age to the global village of which we are all a part. This is a non-threatening and largely apolitical avenue to intercultural awareness. Children who have an intimate knowledge of the songs of more than a single culture come to know—and enjoy—more than one spoken language, one musical language, or one way of looking at the world. This creates within them a sense of welcome and positive recognition when they encounter further diversity, rather than suspicion or hostility. We see this as an important attitude to encourage.

This book and its companion recording are intended as a broad sampling of songs and singing games from an array of cultures on several continents: Africa, Asia, Europe, South America and North America. Previous collections of music of varied cultures have been tailored for older children, lacked in-depth cultural context, had no recording, or did not feature native speakers or culture bearers on the recording. This collection fills the gap in providing songs suitable in both text and music for use with young children, as well as offering them set in cultural context (with a thumbnail sketch of geographic, economic, historical and cultural factors), including maps and brief biographies and photographs of the contributors.

Each song is transcribed in simple melodic musical notation without accompaniment; however, notation is sometimes a difficult and inexact tool to use in communicating the true sound of songs that have so many subtleties of melody, phrasing, tone quality, and rhythm. Use the companion recording freely. It will help you with pronunciation in particular—many of the languages are just about impossible to write out phonetically. In some cases we have given a simplified pronunciation guide, in others, a phonetic version under the transcription, in others a transliteration that will be a bare-bones guide to your listening. Listen to the tape before attempting to use the songs with children, and then listen again with the group. This is your insider's tour of each song. By repeated listening, you and the children will learn the songs with accurate pronunciation and complete with the cultural nuances imbued in the singers' performances. Additional suggestions will encourage you—the teacher, parent, librarian or community outreach worker—to extend the learning process beyond only listening to or singing the songs. Many of the songs are associated with games, gestures and full-body movements that children find so attractive, and that are often vital in gaining and maintaining their attention.

The contributors and performers of these songs are friends, colleagues or students of ours, who were asked to offer some of their earliest and dearest musical memories, or to share a song that might have some important meaning for them or for children. These contributors recognize that an important measure of their personal identity is their cultural identity, molded from the clay of their childhood sights, sounds and mentors. They share in the belief that songs and chants are among the richest of cultural experiences young children can know. Years later, the internal echo of a musical childhood memory resonates in the adult mind and continues to define some aspect of the adult in their present context. Each musical memory has been with these bearers for many years, cherished as a gift of childhood that also was a reminder of their culture. Such songs have "staying power": they are not easily abandoned but dwell deeply within, ready to surface in years to come. They are the whispers of generations past lingering in the inner ears of the present generation.

A very interesting phenomenon came to light as we contacted contributors. For a few, the traditions that have such vital importance for them now were not necessarily learned in their own homes, directly from their parents. The mother tongue of their culture was also not learned from their parents. Due to a variety of reasons, reflected a million times over in the American experience, the parents of one contributor kept the old language strictly as a way to communicate to each other or to the grandparents when they did not want the children understanding the conversation. In another effort to become mainstream American, a family discontinued their cultural holidays and traditions, observing only the holidays of American mass culture. The result was that a couple of our contributors felt a sense of loss and confusion growing up, which they gradually came to realize was the mark of the loss of their cultural identity. A personal odyssey to reclaim their roots and reestablish cultural traditions began in the teen or adult years for these individuals. One made a pilgrimage to the "homeland" and stayed for years. One joined a group of musicians specializing in the music of her ancestors; she gradually re-learned the language, ate the foods, and found new meaning in the holidays. One spent years collecting children's game songs from her heritage, then shared them with her grandparents who delightedly reminded her that when she was very young, some of those very songs were their favorites. In all cases, this successful search for their cultural foundation created in them a sense of completion and wholeness, and a commitment to not allow their heritage to die out in generations to come.

One additional phenomenon, present here in one case, is personal dedication to a music and culture not one's own from birth. It sometimes happens that an individual will become immersed in a cultural context and through study with acknowledged masters and long-term contact with a community, will be adopted into that culture. We feel it is important to present you with this part of the spectrum as well.

Although this set is intended principally for use by those who live or work with children ages 4 through 12, we present this collection to all who enjoy sampling the melodies, rhythms and languages of the world. We have been enriched by these songs, slipping them in among our own longtime favorites. For the child in each of us and for our own children, a broader base of songs to sing and to listen to may bring us more in tune with the global village of our time, and with the multicultural mosaic of neighbors, friends, and fellow citizens around us. These are the roots that anchor us to generations of tradition, these are the branches that intertwine to create a strong network of support, intercultural understanding and mutual respect. This is the legacy we hope to leave today's children through the joy of absorbing these musical gifts.

Africa

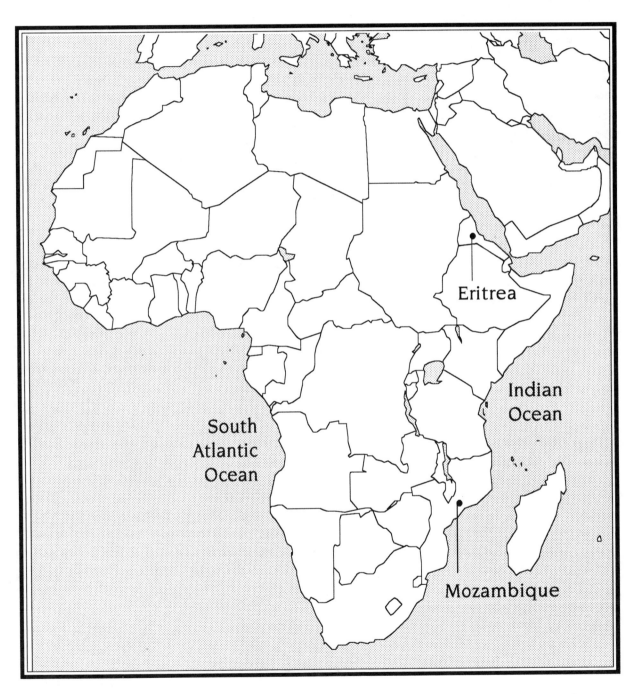

Eritrea

South
Atlantic
Ocean

Indian
Ocean

Mozambique

Eritrea
Mozambique

Eritrea

Hidaat Ephrem and her son Sirak J. Haile

*"In Eritrea,
you sing wherever you are.
I'm used to singing
when I'm walking,
and learned many Eritrean values
through song."*

- Hidaat Ephrem

Hidaat Ephrem was born and raised in Asmara, Eritrea, a small African country bordered by the Red Sea. Her immediate family consisted of five girls and two boys, raised primarily by their mother Haimanot, after their father Ephrem died when he was quite young. Unlike modern American families, that scatter in many directions as the individuals grow up and follow whatever opportunities are presented, Eritreans traditionally stayed fairly close to where they were raised. Hidaat felt very close to her extended family of aunts, uncles and cousins who lived nearby and frequently played together. When Hidaat was a child, there was no telephone in her home, but there was always a warm welcome for friends and relatives who dropped in unannounced for a visit. Likewise, when her own family wanted to visit someone, they would walk over to the home in their neighborhood or farther away, taking the chance that the residents might not be at home when the guests arrived at their door.

Hidaat's home was much like the other lower middle class homes in Eritrea, a simple two-room structure made of stone with an insulated tin roof, and an outside kitchen that was a center of activity. Her mother made a traditional fermented bread, like crepes, out of *taff*, a grain that grows only in that part of the world. Sometimes she would bake bread from the staple grains: wheat, barley or corn. Hidaat loved the plump local dates and tropical fruits, especially mangoes, that were abundant. A small fenced yard gave the family privacy and extended the living space, particularly important in such a hot, dry climate where much daily activity is done outdoors. She had a pet dog with a typical Italian dog-name, "Bobbi," and a white cat affectionately named "Shashu," Whitey.

One surefire way to meet up with friends and relatives was to travel to their neighborhood on the days of the feast of the local saint. In Hidaat's Greek-Orthodox faith, feast days called *negdet* take place on the twenty-first of the month. In Asmara, the local church observes Saint Mary's feast day on November 21. The feast would begin with church members and priests walking through the streets, chanting and singing religious songs. In some of the villages where Hidaat's father came from, January 17 is a *negdet*, and since January is also a popular month for weddings, bridegrooms perform special dances and songs. Everyone comes out, and anxious parents scout the crowds for young women who might be suitable brides for arranged marriages with their sons.

One of Hidaat's strongest memories is of climbing on a little rock beside her house and watching the sun set, while longing to know what might lie in the distance beyond her village. She eventually left Asmara, and in 1972 journeyed to the United States to study broadcast journalism at the University of Minnesota. Later, it turned out it was fortunate she was no longer in the country, because the upheavals created a hellish time of famine and displacement, and misfortune for her family. She and her son, Sirak J. Haile (who also sings on the recording) now live in Seattle, Washington. Hidaat is a poet, writing in English as well as her mother tongue, Tighriyna, and she also speaks Italian and Amharic. She teaches traditional children's songs to the young people in the Eritrean community, to keep her beloved music alive.

Eritrea sits at the northeast tip of the African horn with Ethiopia on the east and Sudan on the south. Its strategic location proved very appealing to foreign aggressors in the past. An Italian colony from 1889 until World War II, Eritrea was forcibly occupied by neighboring Ethiopia in 1951. Following a war that ravaged both countries, in 1993 Eritrea became the independent nation it is today.

Industrialized while still a colony, Eritrea is currently in the vanguard of modern technology. Ancient African tradition and contemporary western style intermingle in Eritrea. Palm trees, tropical flowers, well-manicured lawns and high-rise buildings grace its cities. The boutiques, cafes and movie houses come to life in the cool of the evening. Children learn English as a second language in school, and fluency in Italian is quite common.

Despite its proximity to the Arab world, and despite being a crossroads culture, influenced by trade with India, China, the Middle East and Europe through the Red Sea coast, Eritrea is home to distinctive ethnic groups that retain their traditions and identity even as they selectively adopt Western ways.

Most Eritreans embrace some form of Christianity or Islam—approximately half are Christian, predominantly Greek Orthodox, and perhaps forty percent are Muslims. Most women wear traditional long, gauze dresses and veils to protect themselves from the sun and wind. However, the women of some of the ethnic groups that follow Islam, including the Rashaida who live on the coast of the Red Sea, are extremely strict about the clothing women traditionally wear outside their tent dwellings. Rashaida women and girls over the age of five wear the *burga*, a heavy, embroidered mask of cloth, covered with silver threads and beads, clearly a link to their Middle Eastern history. When Rashaida women marry they wear the *Arusi*, a heavy, jeweled garment decorated with silver and gold that allows only the eyes to show. Women wear jewelry that reveals both how much they are worth (shown by the quantity and quality of the pieces) and also the ethnic group to which they belong (identified by the style of the jewelry).

Ancient wisdom and traditions are preserved and passed on by the spoken word. The history and spirit of the Eritrean people are alive in Tighriyna, Tigre and Arabic, the three dominant languages, and six other languages used by the remaining unique ethnic groups. Firmly grounded in this rich oral tradition, Eritreans understand their world in the phraseology and teachings of the songs, chants, and stories they learned as children. Learning to read and write in the classroom is still a relatively new experience in Eritrea where schools were first established at the turn of the century, by the Italians. Each area has local elementary schools, and there are many junior high schools, but relatively few high schools. All children begin studies in elementary school, but only a few are privileged enough to continue on to finish high school. As in much of northeastern Africa, the illiteracy rate is relatively high.

Singing is very much a part of school life. Children learn to get along with and respect others, to work hard, and to express their joys and sorrows largely through unaccompanied song. A strong voice and pair of clapping hands are the most popular instruments.

The *kirar* is a popular five-string instrument similar to a guitar, hand-crafted by musicians who play them. The *keboro*, a round two-headed drum with a sling that goes over the player's right shoulder, allowing him to play and dance at the same time.

Eritreans enjoy singing and dancing together, yet music is also encouraged for individual self-expression. Music is thoroughly integrated in the community, as much a part of life as breathing—Eritreans sing to celebrate a new life or to mourn a death, and for all that comes in between.

⌐All about
Kumbraza

*Tortoise,
your mom wants you!*

"**K**umbraza," which means tortoise in Tighriyna, is one of the best-known Eritrean children's songs. Hidaat learned the song from other children in her family and neighborhood when she was about four years old. Typical of many songs in Eritrea and northeastern Africa, "Kumbraza" is sung in call and response form. A leader sings a solo part, followed by a group response. While singing, one of the participants imitates the turtle. Wearing a towel over his head to suggest a shell, the child holds a stick to suggest the turtle's head. He moves the stick back and forth to the rhythmic pulse of the slow-moving tortoise. The song urges the tortoise to go to the backyard because he is wanted there by his mother.

Lyrics:
Ati kumbraza-ye, kumbraza (solo)
Kumbraza (group)
Ati kumbraza-ye, kumbraza (solo)
Kumbraza (group)
Adiechi mesee-a dihri geza, kumbraza (solo)
Kumbraza (group)

Translation:
Hey, Tortoise, tortoise
Tortoise
Hey tortoise, tortoise
Tortoise
Your mom is in the backyard
Tortoise

✺ Extensions

1. Listen to the recording and sing along. (Note that when sung, the word *kumbraza* sounds like kum*bara*za. The transcription is written as it sounds.) Clap on the pulse and sway from right to left to feel the beat.

2. Ask the children to move as slowly as a tortoise, or turtle. Sing or play the song, lightly tapping the pulse on a drum. In the song, the tortoise is being called by his mother to the backyard, and so, since he would rather play with his friends, he moves reluctantly in her direction. The children can imitate the turtle's slow progress.

3. Have one child play the tortoise at a time. Place a long stick between the child's hands, and a scarf over his or her head. The slow movements of the tortoise are made by rubbing the stick between the hands, which moves the scarf. The other children clap on the pulse and sing. They will be both delighted and intrigued by the "mystery" of the moving scarf.

Kumbraza
(Tortoise)

Moderate Swing   (x = clap)

(Leader) At-i kum ba ra-za ye — — Kum-ba-ra - za kum-ba-ra-
(Chorus)

za. (Leader) At-i kum ba-ra-za ye — — Kum-ba-ra - za Kum-ba ra-
(Chorus)

za (Leader) Ade-chi me-see-a — — — di-hri ge - za kum-ba-ra-za
(Chorus)

All about

Hashewie

Going Round

✍ Extensions

"**H**ashewie" is a song popular with Eritreans of all ages. Men, women, and children compose their own personal versions of "Hashewie" to express personal or political feelings. They refer to "my Hashewie" and "your Hashewie."

A leader sings his or her part, to which a group of singers respond. The creativity of the lead singer is displayed in expressive text spontaneously created to fit the melody. People hold hands in a circle, singing while stepping to the pulse. Hidaat Ephrem composed the text to the "Hashewie" below, which has special appeal to children in an Eritrean-American community.

Lyrics:
Hashewie (solo), Shewie (group) [three times]
Bihade habirna (solo), Shewie (group)
Hashewie enabelna (solo), Shewie (group)
Alem Kitfelto (solo), Shewie (group)
Kulu meninetna (solo), Shewie (group)
Hashewie nibel (solo), Shewie (group)
Nefalt adina (solo), Shewie (group)
Hashewie (solo), Shewie (group) [three times]

Translation:
Going round and round, round (three times)
All together, round
Saying round, round
So the world would know, round
Who we are, round
Let's say, round
All together, round
Going round and round, round (three times)

1. Say the word *shewie*, and then sing it. *Shewie* means "round" in Tihgriyna. In the context of the song, *hashewie* means "going round and round."

2. Stand in a circle with one participant singing the leader's part (*hashewie*) and cue the others to sing the response (*shewie*). First clap the pulse while standing and singing, then continue to sing while moving to the right, stepping the pulse.

3. Once the melody is familiar, invent some new words to sing (in English) to express thoughts about the weather, children within the group, items on the news. In Eritrea, this song allows people to express themselves. It can even convey news and current events where there is no television or newspaper. Encourage the invention of short phrases to which the group can respond "shewie."

Hashewie
(Going Round)

Mozambique

Salomao Manhica

*"I love music, and always have.
I remember that
one of my cousins had worked
in the gold mines of South Africa
(in the 1950s,
men from Mozambique were
initiated into adulthood
by going off to work for a time
in the mines),
and when he came back,
he played the guitar
and sang for us.
I remember thinking,
'When I grow up, I want to do
music the way he does'."*

- Salomao Manhica

Salomao Manhica was born in a small village 30 miles from Maputo. A deeply motivated scholar, he simultaneously studied law at the University of Lisbon and music at the National Conservatory of Music in Portugal. His professional résumé reflects the diversity of his educational pursuits, holding positions that include chief of staff for the Minister of Justice in Mozambique, head of the Department of Education and Culture for the Armed Forces, and head of the Department of Cultural Affairs in the Mozambican Ministry of Education and Culture.

As a member of the Mozambique liberation movement in 1974, he collected numerous songs which inspired his fellow freedom fighters. Composer as well as anthologist, he wrote and recorded three collections of songs, including the Mozambican Women's Anthem. Many of these pieces, born of the struggle for freedom, have become symbols for the nation's patriotism and are performed on national holidays. He arrived in the United States in 1988, to study for a Ph.D. in ethnomusicology at the University of Washington.

Mozambique is located on the southeastern coast of Africa. After several centuries of Arab influence, it was colonized and settled by the Portuguese in 1492. At first just the coastal area was settled, with penetration to the interior following much later. The expanse of Swahili and Arab influence essentially ends in the north of Mozambique. The area's Makonde people are noted for their rich sculpture and masked dances. In the south, near the capital city of Maputo, live the Thonga group who speak the languages of Ronga, Shangana, Tswa, and Tsonga. Mozambique is an ethnically-complex country that is home to many other groups, some of whom have come from the neighboring countries of Zimbabwe, Zambia, Tanzania, and South Africa.

Mozambique was liberated from Portugal only recently, in 1975. Portuguese is still the official language for education, government, and business. It is spoken nationwide in addition to six major mother-tongue languages and approximately thirty dialects. There is a trend towards English becoming the language of choice among students, who favor it

Salomao Manhica and his family playing their xylophones

already for the practical reason that most of Mozambique's neighbors already conduct business and trade in English.

Secondary school students in the cities are increasingly looking to study at European and American universities, although the majority of children in the rural areas continue to absorb the age-old traditions and culture of their families and communities.

Mozambique enjoys one of the richest mosaics of musical tradition in all of Africa, owing to the slow rate of urbanization and development, and the Portuguese tolerance of folk arts. The Chopi people are internationally-known for their xylophone orchestras, and the government is moving towards establishing theirs as the national music of Mozambique. In addition to this strong xylophone tradition, there are also superb drummers who play stylistically diverse music on instruments of many sizes

and shapes. Bone, wood, and bamboo flutes, ocarinas of gourd or clay, and panpipes contribute to their communal melodies as do one-string musical bows, and board zithers. The men traditionally play the instruments as the women sing. Their voices are typically strong and piercing enough to be heard, even above the thick polyphonic texture of the instrumental ensembles.

Both men and women yodel in central Mozambique. Men in the south perform in vocal dance groups, singing the songs they first developed while working in the South African mines. Mining authorities forbade their workers from drumming, fearful of the strength and capacity for communication inherent in the instrument. With indestructible spirit much in evidence, the miners soon developed songs and dances in which they played their traditional drum rhythms on their high rubber gumboots!

Yo Mamana Yo

Oh, Mama!

A popular children's lullaby of the Ronga and Shangana people in the southern provinces is "Yo Mamana Yo." Women sing it to their babies and children not only to lull them to sleep, but also to calm and soothe their crying if they are hurt or distressed. The Ronga word for mother is *mamana*. The song is accompanied by a rocking or swaying movement to suit the rhythm of the melody.

Lyrics:
Yo mamana yo,
Yo mamana yo,
Unga famba uni siya.
Uni siyela vusiwana.

Translation:
Oh, mama.
Oh, mama.
You left me alone,
With my suffering.

∾ Extensions

1. Listen for any words that may sound familiar. Explain that *yo mamana* is a way of calling one's mother in the Ronga language. Note the similarity of *mamana* to "mama."

2. Pat the first of three pulses in each measure on your lap. Gently, pat two fingers on the lap for beat 1 and then into the palm of the other hand for beats 2 and 3, keep the rhythm of the beat: *pat lap   tap   tap*
                                    1   2   3

3. Form a circle with joined hands and sway from right to left, with one swaying movement for every three pulses.

Yo, Mamana, Yo

(Oh, Mama, Oh)

Moderate Sway

Yo ma - ma-na yo,   Yo ma - ma-na yo,

Un - ga fam-ba u - ni si - ya.   U - ni si-ye-la vusi-wa - na.

Tenho uma boneca

I Have A Doll

"Tenho uma boneca" is a popular children's song known throughout Mozambique. The Portuguese text renders it universally understandable and a good choice for radio transmission. Children sing it in kindergarten and in elementary school, clapping hands and/or jumping rhythmically to the pulse. They may also imitate the movement of the doll's head from side to side. When the song is heard (each night) on the radio at 8 PM, children know it's time to get ready for bed!

Portuguese Pronunciation

- "a" = f*a*r,

- "e" = h*ey*, or m*ee*t

- "i" = m*ee*t, "o" = b*oo* or g*o*

- "s" before o =z; at end of word = sh

- "z" = mea*s*ure

Lyrics:
Tenho uma boneca
Assim, assim!
Veio de Inhambane,
P'ra mim, p'ra mim!
Ela diz "papa"
"Mama" tambem!
Ela fecha os olhos
E dorme ben.

Translation:
I have a doll
Like this, like this!
She came from Inhambane (southern coastal city)
To me, to me!
She says "papa"
And "mama" too!
She closes her eyes
And sleeps well!

∾ Extensions

1. This song is about a doll from Mozambique, but traditionally, words might also be inserted to indicate a teddy bear, dog, or other favorite stuffed animal.

2. Find the Portuguese words for mama and papa. Learn and use these simple phrases in Portuguese: *Dorme ben*, which means "sleep well" (like saying "good night") and *assim*, which means "like this."

3. Form a circle and sing, clapping to the beat. Other movements to the beat may include moving side to side from right to left, walking around the circle, or dancing like a doll or stuffed animal. Children also enjoy moving their favorite dolls or stuffed animals to the beat.

Tenho Uma Boneca

(I Have A Doll)

Ten-ho u-ma bo-ne-ca As - sim, as- sim! Ve- io de In-ham-ba-ne, P'ra

mim, p'ra mim! E - la diz 'pa-pa', 'Ma- ma' tam - bem!

E - la fesh-a os ol -hos E dor - me ben.

Section 2
Asia

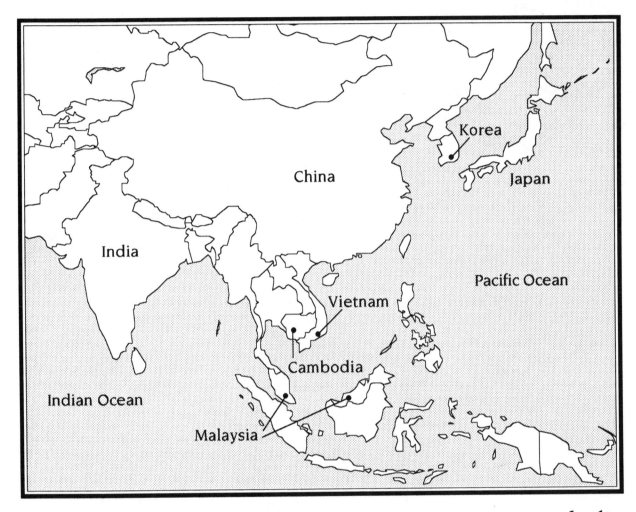

Cambodia
China
India
Japan
Korea
Malaysia
Vietnam

Cambodia

Sam-Ang Sam

*"In Cambodia,
some songs for children
are often intended by adults
to teach them about nature,
birds and animals,
good manners and hygiene,
and respect for elders.
But I also remember
watching and learning traditional
singing games
that were played by older children
in my village, and in
the nearby temple compounds
during the
New Year celebrations."*

- Sam-Ang Sam

Sam-Ang Sam is one of the few Khmer master musicians who survived the terrible years of the Pol Pot regime. Born in Krakor (in Pursat province in west central Cambodia), he showed a strong interest in music from early childhood, and began his formal studies of instrumental and vocal music when he was 14. It is common in Cambodia for children to choose the instruments they want to learn, and Sam-Ang became acquainted with several different types which he studied formally and informally, including the *roneat* xylophone, a favorite of music students, *khloy*, a bamboo end-blown flute, and later, the *sralai*, a quadruple-reed shawm made of hardwood or ivory, which became his primary instrument.

In the course of becoming a Khmer musician, every student must apprentice to a teacher or teachers, and move through a long period of study guided firmly by the teacher. Young people do not simply sign up for lessons at the local music store! The potential student is introduced to the teacher, and then needs to prove his/her commitment, courtesy, respect and patience before the relationship is formalized through a ceremony call *sampeah krou* (salute the teacher). Sam-Ang often brought gifts for his teachers, including money, fruits and cakes. Traditionally, Cambodian music is passed orally from teacher to student, without the use of notation even as a reference. This is one reason why the program of genocide by Pol Pot, which decimated the numbers of artists and musicians, was particularly devastating.

He earned degrees from the University of Fine Arts in Phnom Penh and received his Ph.D. in ethnomusicology from Wesleyan University in Connecticut. A scholar of Khmer music, he has written several books and articles on the subject. He, his wife, dancer Chan Moly Sam, and children are sought-after performers of Khmer traditional music and dance in the United States, Europe, and Asia, and he has has released several recordings. He is currently in Washington, D.C., where he is actively engaged in projects with Cambodian refugee groups.

Cambodia is a Southeast Asian country about the size of the state of Washington. Thailand, Laos, and Vietnam are its neighbors. Nearly 10% of Cambodia's area is made up of water or marshland. Significant waterways include the Mekong and Bassac rivers, and the Tonle Sap or "Great Lake." The Gulf of Siam forms its southern boundary.

Tigers, leopards, wild elephants, rhinoceroses, wild oxen and buffalo are among the many animals which live in this lush country. A farming nation producing four rice crops a year, almost 90% of Cambodia's inhabitants still engage in agricultural pursuits. The fishing industry is second in importance to the economy, followed by the tapping of its rubber trees for export.

About 85% of the population of Cambodia is Khmer, a group that is the result of many centuries of cultural blending. The Vietnamese and Chinese living in Cambodia each constitute about seven percent of the population. Other smaller minority groups include Thais and Laotians who have lived side-by-side with the Khmer for centuries. (Formerly used to describe the dominant ethnic group, the term "Khmer" now designates nationality.) Legends, as well as inscriptions on ancient monuments and temples such as Angkor Vatt, tell the story of the Khmer people and the many contenders for their rich and fertile land. Fragmented records found in Cambodia, China, India, and much later, France give detail to the story. The Khmer culture was at its peak during the Angkor Period. From 802 B.C. -1432 A.D. its influence spread throughout much of Thailand, Laos, Vietnam, and the Malay peninsula. Struggling to maintain a national identity through several successive centuries, the Khmer Empire finally appealed to France in the nineteenth century for protection against aggression by neighboring nations. The political situation in Cambodia has been unstable in recent decades, especially during the genocidal rule of the Khmer Rouge under the leadership of Pol Pot. Many musicians, artists, dancers and intellectuals were killed, taking their knowledge (which in many cases was never written down) to their graves. Many Cambodian refugees fled their homeland to seek peace in Australia, New Zealand, Japan, France, the United States, Canada, and Europe.

Temple carvings immortalize the musicians and dancers of Cambodia's royal courts. The tradition of court dances, with graceful hand and finger motions dense with meaning, and masked plays requires years of intensive training, begun in early childhood, to mold and prepare the dancer's body for the intricate choreography. Costuming for these dances is an art form in itself, combining elaborate design in cloth as well as gilded masks. The country's musical heritage is kept alive at the University of Fine Arts, and through lessons offered in Cambodian cultural centers abroad. Significant Cambodian instruments include wooden xylophones known as *roneat*, sets of knobbed gongs set in a circular frame (*korng tauch*), the *khloy* flute, two- and three-stringed *tror* fiddles, and a variety of percussion instruments. The *krapeau*, (meaning "crocodile") is a long, three-stringed zither with a body or board resonator the shape of a crocodile. It is plucked with a small piece of buffalo horn or ivory tied to the player's index finger with string.

Music is a prominent feature of the traditional Khmer New Year celebration in April. This is called *Chaul Chhnaim* in Khmer, and takes place during April 13-15, at a time and date calculated by astrologers. Khmer in Cambodia spend the entire month previous in preparation for the celebration, decorating their houses with candles, lights, star-shaped lanterns, and flowers. Celebrants make pilgrimages to pagodas during the first three days of the lunar year, to pray for prosperity, good health, show appreciation to their parents and elders, and offer food to the monks. Like New Year's celebrants everywhere, Cambodians make resolutions, and also pay debts and exchange gifts. There is lots of dancing and games for all ages to enjoy during *Chaul Chhnaim*.

Music is also important during the Flower Ceremony (*Bonn Phka*) which raises funds to support local monasteries, and at the September honoring of deceased relatives and ancestors called *Phchum Benn*.

An exciting and unusual setting for musical performance is at the boxing matches. Boxing is the most popular sport in Cambodia. The matches attract large, mostly male, audiences, who are grouped around three sides of the ring. The judges sit on the fourth side, and the musicians sit at the back or are in a balcony area. There is only one piece played for boxing matches, commonly referred to as "Phleng Pradall." The performers play the *sralai* quadruple-reed shawm, *sampho* drum and finger-sized gongs called *chhing*. The boxers prepare for the fight by pantomiming movements during the first part of the piece, and then use the second part of the music to guide their jumps, kicks and jabs during the fight itself. Boxing in Cambodia is like dancing, and music is key to the sport.

⌐All about
Leak Kanseng

Hide The Scarf

From an early age, Khmer children enjoy the singing game called "Leak Kanseng." Sam-Ang often played the game with his friends in their village of Bamnak. It is seen and heard especially at the time of special holidays such as New Year, the Soul of Ancestors Day in September, and the Flower Ceremony in October. In Cambodia, a favorite place to play a game like "Leak Kanseng" is an open space such as a a temple yard or school yard. The boys and girls gather in a circle, and one makes a tied bundle out of a rectangular scarf that is similar to the traditional silk or cotton *krama*. (The larger lengths of *krama* are worn as informal garments. Women wear the *krama* diagonally across the chest, men wear the *krama* wrapped around their hip when they work or bathe. It is a very versatile cloth that can be wrapped around the head to protect it from sun, or twisted into a tight rope and shaped into a circle, then placed on the head like a crown so that big pots or baskets of fruit will balance easily for carrying.) Sam-Ang remembers other traditional Khmer games that use bundled scarves—not unusual since scarves are part of the traditional clothing, and so it is likely someone in a group will have at least one handy!

Lyrics (transliteration):
Leak kanseng!
Chhma khaim keng!
Oh long oh long.

Translation:
Hide the scarf!
The cat is biting his/her heel!
And drags the leg.

➳ Extensions

1. Sing the song. Call attention to the "limping" rhythm (♪. ♪) of the opening pitches, which could well be the movement of the scarf-hider whose leg has been bitten by the large cat (tiger).

2. Play the game while singing the song, using the directions on the next page.

3. There are many traditional scarf games found in other cultures such as "Blind Man's Bluff," "Flag Tag," "Pin the Tail on the Donkey," "Little Johnny Brown" (African-American), and "Xay Khan" (Vietnamese). Perhaps a child in the group knows one of these or another to share.

Leak Kanseng
Hide The Scarf

Leak kan seng chhma khaim keng oh long oh long.

Game Directions:

• One child with a scarf walks around the outside of the circle, as those within the circle sing the chant.

• The "scarf-hiding" child drops the scarf as unobtrusively as possible behind another child's back. This child must be very alert to realize the "scarf hider" no longer has the scarf in hand.

• S/he picks it up and chases the one who dropped it around the outside of the circle.

• Usually, the scarf-hider makes it back to the sitting child's vacated spot in the circle, so that the game begins anew with the former sitting child as the new scarf-hider.

[A variation might be that if the "scarf-hider" is tagged by the other child in the chase, s/he remains in that role. A possible scenario is that the sitting child may not notice that the scarf was dropped behind him. In this case the "scarf-hider" picks the scarf up as s/he comes around again, and places the scarf behind a new child.]

∽All about
Sarika Keo

The Sariko Keo Bird

Sam-Ang learned "Sarika Keo" from the primary school teacher in his village when he was very young. He enjoyed it so much he never forgot it, and taught it to his own children as soon as they could learn it. They, in turn, taught it to their friends. The song is very popular in Cambodia and in Cambodian-American communities because it portrays an important part of Khmer life: the small black bird with white and yellow markings on its head called *sarika keo*. The bird symbolizes nature in all of its beauty and color, and it is said to be among the most beautiful of all birds. The Khmer enjoy training the *sarika keo* bird to speak such phrases as "Teou na?" (Where are you going?) and "Arkun" (Thank you). There are other birds of many colors living in wooded areas and tall grasses of the Mekong River Delta, including the *sek*, *moan prey*, *popich*, and *lolork*. Some of these are domesticated and are enjoyed as pets. As children in Cambodia learn the song, they learn also about the bird, how it eats, plays, sings and dances.

Lyrics (transliteration):
Solo: Sarika keo euy si ey kang kang? ⎤
Response: Ey sariyaing. ⎦2X
Solo:Si phle dambang prachoeuk knea leng.
Response: Euy keo keo euy.] 2X

Solo:Slap vea chakk kbach moat vea thveu phleng.
Response: Ey sariyaing.] 2X
Solo:Prachoeuk knea leng leu mek proeuksa.
Response: Euy keo keo euy.] 2X

Translation:
(Girls) Oh! Sarika keo, what are you eating?
(Boys) [Vocables]
(Girls) You are eating cactus fruits,
You are playfully nipping at each other.
(Boys) [Vocables]

(Boys) With your wing you dance,
With your beak you sing.
(Girls)[Vocables]
(Boys) You nip at each other, on the tree branch.
(Girls)[Vocables]

∾ Extensions

1. Listen to the recording, and see if the children are able to pick out the responsive phrases that indicate the bird's call: *ey sariyaing* and *euy keo keo euy*.

2. The song may be sung alternately by girls and boys, with the other group responding with the untranslatable

vocables. As in Cambodia, even very young children can be divided to listen to the polysyllabic lines and then to sing only the brief responses that say the bird's calls. These vocables are meant to sound like the call of the *sarika keo* bird. Teach the responses "Ey sariyaing" and "Euy keo keo euy." Sing or play the song, cuing children to sing the responses.

2. Give the translation of the song. The Khmer word for bird is *bakkha* (or sometimes *baksa*). The children will enjoy talking about and imitating the songs and movements of familiar birds they have observed.

3. There are many songs about birds. Some might be known to children in the group, e.g. "When the Red Red Robin Comes Bob, Bob, Bobbin' Along," "The Cuckoo is a Pretty Bird," "Turtle Dove Done Drooped His Wing," and "Blue Bird, Blue Bird at My Window."

Sarika Keo
(*The Sarika Keo Bird*)

Sari - ka keo euy si ey kang kang ey sari - yaing sari - ka keo

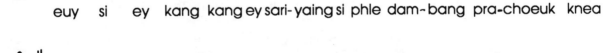

euy si ey kang kang ey sari - yaing si phle dam - bang pra-choeuk knea

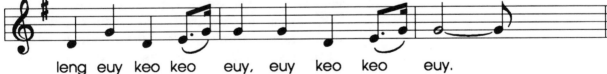

leng euy keo keo euy, euy keo keo euy.

China

Ling Tong and her daughter, Ran

*"Before the Cultural Revolution
we heard and learned
Chinese folk songs
from the radio, from school
and from our families.
During the Cultural Revolution
we only sang these songs
in the privacy of our own homes.
Folk songs
were considered 'bourgeois'."*

- Ling Tong

Ling Tong was raised in Qingdao, a northeastern Chinese coastal city. She sang quite a bit as a child, even performing on the radio at age four. Her mother, who played the piano and had a lovely singing voice taught Ling many old ballads and songs. Ling began the violin at age 8, taking private lessons until she was 14. Her teacher was persecuted at this time by the Cultural Revolution and private lessons were no longer allowed.

Ling remembers the terror she felt when her home was searched twice by the Red Guard. Everything considered "bourgeois" had to be destroyed, including books, photos, dresses and art work. Even her father's ties were thrown away. Ling would get up at 5:00 AM to go out on the streets to try to get rid of their books. It was safer for a young child to be out than for adults, who might attract more notice. She remembers many hours spent cutting up her pretty clothes to provide evidence that she had nothing fancy left.

Ling attended college in China, graduating with a B.A. in English. A sponsor she met there supported her immigration to the United States where she attended Brigham Young University, receiving a graduate certificate in English as a Second Language. She also earned an M.A. degree in American Studies from the University of New Mexico, and now lives in Santa Fe where she teaches a course in Chinese cilivization. Her daughter is bilingual and learning calligraphy, and Ling is also teaching her traditional Chinese values including respect of elders. They celebrate important Chinese holidays at a local restaurant with the small Chinese community in Santa Fe, and cook Chinese style daily. Her American husband is an attorney, and they maintain a home with one foot planted firmly in her Chinese heritage, and one striding forward into the American experience.

China (the People's Republic of China) is a vast country with the largest population of any in the world, over *one billion* people. Once called The Middle Kingdom because the Chinese believed themselves to be at the very center of the world, China actually shares land borders with thirteen other countries including Korea, Mongolian People's Republic, Commonwealth of Independent States (formerly the USSR), Afghanistan, Pakistan, India, Bhutan, Nepal, Burma, Laos, Vietnam, and Hong Kong. In addition it has coastal borders on the Yellow, East China and South China Seas.

About 94% of the people in China are Han, descendents of the great Han dynasty. (The remaining 6% is composed of 55 distinct national minorities.) One commonality among the Han people is their written language. Over 2,000 years old and consisting of characters that represent words, one must be able to recognize at least 3,000 characters in order to read Mandarin Chinese, the national language. Spoken Mandarin is tonal, which means that different stresses or inflections can completely change the meaning of a word.

The Chinese are known as the inventors of the magnetic compass, gunpowder, paper and printing. Significant Chinese exports include silk and other textiles, agricultural products and tea, raw materials and electronics.

Following a lengthy series of dynasties and a violent revolution, the People's Republic of China was formed on October 1, 1949, led by Chairman Mao Zedong. Ruling from 1966-1976, Mao initiated the ten-year Cultural Revolution, a tremendous upheaval of the economy, belief systems and life style of the Chinese people. Prior to the revolution, China was plagued by periods of severe famine, and economic injustices. The Revolution was an attempt to balance the situation, yet went to an extreme, seeking to create uniformity of thought and privilege, denouncing and destroying everything considered "bourgeois," and hit artists and intellectuals particularly hard.

Chinese music is well integrated into daily life, and sometimes expressive of Chinese philosophical preoccupations. In the third century B.C. the Chinese categorized musical instruments according to the eight materials from which they were made: metal, stone, silk, bamboo, gourd, pottery, leather, and wood. The use of 5-tone scales is very common in Chinese music, although other scales are used as well.

Classical Chinese instruments, all played in the popular Chinese theatre, include the *qin* (a seven-string zither), the *pipa* (pear-shaped lute), *sheng* (mouth organ), *erhu* (two-stringed violin) and *dizi* (seven-hole bamboo flute). The theater is famous for its flamboyant, exaggerated style. Best known of the theater styles is the Peking (Beijing) Opera. Acrobats, singers, dancers and mimes all perform in highly stylized plays that also employ exaggerated speech and elaborate make-up and costumes. Children begin training for a career in theater by learning a variety of traditional instruments, practicing vocal styles, studying make-up and costuming techniques, and train intensively in acrobatics.

These theatrical skills figure prominently in holiday celebrations. The traditional Chinese calendar is based on the moon, so the date for the new year, Yüan Tan, is not fixed and falls sometime between January 21st and February 19th. A time of great festivity, people celebrate with processions led by enormous dragon figures which weave their way through the streets, accompanied by dancers, acrobats and clowns. The dragon is the Chinese symbol for good fortune, and firecrackers are set off as he passes to "scare off evil spirits." The dragons are actually giant puppets made of bamboo covered in paper or silk and supported from the underside by as many as fifty people. Red is considered a lucky color and children receive New Year gifts of coins wrapped in red paper. Asian communities in the United States celebrate the holiday in the traditional way and children shriek in delight as Chinese-American dragons make their way down the streets of New York and San Francisco.

Celebrated with music, poetry and feasting, the Chinese harvest festival, Chung-Ch'iu honors the moon and its influence on crops, rainfall and harvest. At Chung-Ch'iu time bakeries and confectioners offer large, round moon cakes, and other delicacies prepared in round shapes to honor the celestial orb. The moon is said to be the dwelling place of the immortals who live in great palaces there. Legend has it, that on the night of Chung-Ch'iu, beautiful flowers fall from the moon and all who see them will be especially blessed.

Hao Peng You

Looking For A Friend

"Hao Peng You" is a popular circle game for young children. It is a perfect way to encourage children to get to know each other at the beginning of the school year. (The song is accompanied on the recording by the *erhu*, a two-stringed Chinese violin. Unlike the Western violin, the *erhu* has a hexagonal, octagonal or tubular shaped resonator covered with snake skin, usually python, and a long, round, skinny neck made out of hardwood. The *erhu* bow is made out of horsehair connected to a bamboo stem, rosined on both sides, and placed *between* the two strings. An inward pressure on the bow sounds the low string, an outward pressure is used to play the high string. Different notes are created by placing the fingers gently on the strings without touching the fingerboard.)

Lyrics:
Zhao ya zhao ya zhao ya zhao,
Zhao dao ye ge hao peng you ya,
Jing ge li ya, jiu ge gong ya,
Xiao xi xi ya, wo wo shou ya,
Da jia yi qui, da jia yi qui, tiao wu,
Zhai jian!

Translation:
Looking, looking, looking, looking,
I have found a good friend.
Salute, bow,
Smile and shake hands.
Let's dance together, together.
Good-bye!

Extensions

1. Many traditional Chinese folk songs that are accompanied by an instrument produce a heterophonic texture with the instrument or voice slightly embellishing the melody. In this song, the *erhu* and voice are in unison.

2. The Chinese language is tonal. The inflection of the words is very important. A different inflection may create a word with an entirely different meaning!

3. Pat or step the beat to the music. It is interesting to hear that the two-note melody pattern is repeated many times in the middle section.

Hao Peng You
(Looking For A Friend)

Zhao ya zhao ya zhao ya zhao, zhao dao ye ge hao peng you ya,
[j(ow) yah j(ow) yah   j(ow) yah j(ow) j(ow) t(ow) yee geh h(ow) puhng you yah

jing ge li ya, jiu ge gong ya, xiao xi xi ya, wo wo shou ya,
cheen kuh lee yah jooee kuh koon yah sheeow shee shee yah wuh wuh shoh yah

da jia yi qui, da jia yi qui tiao wu, (Spoken) zhai jian!
dah cheeah yee chee dah cheeah yee chee tee(ow) woo tsay tee en]

Playing the game:

• Children stand in a circle and one child is chosen to be "It."

• "It" moves with a step-hop motion, alternating feet around the circle in a counterclockwise direction. (R step / R hop; L step / L hop—count 1 & 2 &)

Note: If "It" is a girl, the back of her hands touch her waist as she moves. If "It" is a boy, his hands hold his waist.

• At the end of the song "It" stops in front of a child and adds the child to the "It" line. The new child holds onto "Its" shoulders with his/her hands and makes a "train" formation.

• Sing the song over and over until "It" has chosen all of the children in the circle. As each new child is selected the new child is added to the end of the train.

31

Diou Shou Juan'er

Hiding a Handkerchief

"Diou Shou Juan'er is another popular circle game for young children. This song is also accompanied on the recording by the *erhu*.

Lyrics (transliteration):
Diou shou juan'er, diou shou juan'er,
qing qing di fang xai xiao peng you di hou bian,
Da jia bu yao gao su ta,
Kai dain'er, kai dain'er, zhua zhu ta.

Approximate pronunciation:
Dee-oh shoh-ho jehr, dee-oh shoh-ho jehr
cheeng cheeng duh fuhng tsai shee-ow puhng yee-oh
duh hoh mee-ehn
Dah tee-ah boo ee-ah koh soo tah
Kway-dehr kway-dehr jua joo tah.

Translation:
Hiding a handkerchief, hiding a handkerchief,
Lightly, lightly,
Put it at the behind of a little friend,
No one should tell him (her).
Quickly, quickly catch him (her).

❧ Extensions

1. Identify the *erhu* as the accompanying instrument. As in "Looking for a Friend," the *erhu* plays an introduction, accompanies the singer and does an instrumental interlude between verses.

2. Pat the beat. Note that in measure five there is a syncopated rhythmic pattern which is very typically Chinese.

Ling Tong as a child

Diou Shou Juan'er

(Hiding a Handkerchief)

Diou shou juan'er, diou shou juan'er,

qing qing di fang xai xiao peng you di hou bian,

Da jia bu yao gao su ta,

Kai dain'er, kai dain'er, zhua zhu ta.

Playing the game:

• Children sit on the floor in a circle formation. One child is selected to be "It."

• "It" has a handkerchief and walks around the circle to the beat. "It" drops the handkerchief behind a child's back and starts to run.

• The instant the child in the circle discovers that the handkerchief is behind his/her back, the child chases "It." "It" tries to sit down in the chaser's place before getting caught.

• If "It" is caught, "It" has to give a "performance" such as jumping up and down or mimicking an erhu player in the middle of the circle. In either case, the "chaser" is "It" the next time.

• The children in the circle clap to the beat all the way through the song when singing. The song usually stops when the "chaser" starts to run after "It." The children are just too excited to continue singing! This song is very much like the "Drop the Handkerchief" and "Duck, Duck, Goose" games played by children in the United States.

India

Shanta Benegal as a baby

Shanta Benegal was born in Mangalore on the west coast of India, and grew up in Bombay. Her mother-tongue is Konkani, but she also speaks Marathi, Hindi, and English. Her formal study of classical Hindustani vocal music began as an adult, but as a young child she enjoyed singing songs associated with melodic structures called *raga*. Today she is an information specialist for the School of Music and the Department of Dance at the University of Washington.

Her mother often sang "Dhahee Maatyaar" to her little brother as a lullaby. She learned "Baariye Bubly" as a member of an after-school children's club in Bombay called *Balodahyan*, the Garden of Children. Shanta Benegal sings and plays the four-stringed drone instrument called the *tambura*.

*"In school,
our teacher would send us
to the music teacher
and plead with her
to create music to help us learn and
memorize poems,
and mathematical concepts.
My first memory
of learning anything
are the multiplication tables,
which we sang
to an Indian rag (melody).
Ever since my school days, memory
is closely linked
to melody."*

- Shanta Benegal

India is a vast country, peninsular in shape, which stretches over 2,000 miles from its southern tip to the Himalayan Mountains in the north. Culturally diverse, the country is populated by members of many ethnic groups and religions. Over 80% of the people adhere closely to the tenets of Hinduism, which flavors the literature and legendary music, dance, and architecture of the sub-continent. The names of some of the major languages spoken here sound themselves like poetry - Hindi, Bengali, Tamil, Telugu, Marathhi, Gujarati, Urdu, Punjabi, and the pan-Indian English language. In addition, there are more than 300 mother-tongues and local dialects too numerous to mention.

India's cuisine is often hot and spicy, featuring mouth watering curries and dishes made with yogurt, cucumbers, coconut and aromatic Basmati rice. It is not unusual for people to follow a vegetarian diet, owing to the great variety of fruits and vegetables available. Children enjoy water buffalo milk. In traditional Indian homes people cook their rice to be on the sticky side, just the right consistency to eat out of hand. Banana leaves are used for plates and the Basmati rice is formed with the fingers into small balls which are used to pick up other bits of food. Finger bowls of water delicately scented with flower petals are set out at each place so diners may clean their hands. It is a common practice after banquets for the banana leaves with bits and pieces of food still on them to be distributed to the poor so that nothing goes to waste, as India is still dealing with great poverty among many of its people.

India's city streets are lively with street musicians playing reed flutes and conical or goblet shaped drums, snake charmers who mesmerize their basket-dwelling reptiles with their gourd-and-double- pipe instruments, and by people singing as they make they way among the merchants offering grains, rice, vegetables, fruits, cotton and silk materials. At home and in restaurants, the All-India Radio broadcasts programs of Indian classical music to entertain young and old alike, and favorite tapes of classical and pop music are played, exchanged with friends, and replayed.

Capacity audiences pack theatres which feature movie musicals in which the movie stars sing and dance; their songs are learned by ear and sung long after the the film has left town. For those who can manage the price of a ticket, the classical music concert scene in cities like Bombay, Delhi, Madras, and Calcutta is a lively one, particularly in the cooler season from November through February. For all Indians, music is a vital component of their daily lives. Perhaps the best known musicians outside of India are Ravi Shankar and Ali Akbar Khan who have both toured widely and taught in the United States.

Education is valued in India, and all children have access to formal education through secondary school. For a long while in India, the first level of schooling was referred to as "the infant class." Six-year-olds attended this class before promotion to class one and two, the equivalent of grades one and two in the United States.

Children learn by oral recitation in the early grades. They listen to their teacher recite a factual statement (concerning a grammatical rule, an historical truth, or a mathematical principle, for example) and then repeat it. A melody is often added to the statements to facilitate memorization. The result is that Indian children often grow up to be highly verbal as well as musical, retaining much of what they were orally taught.

Those who show musical promise and are willing to practice great discipline and dedication to their musical studies might undertake training with a revered master musician. The master musicians include singers and dancers of various styles as well as instrumental virtuosi on stringed instruments such as the violin and *sitar*, *vina*, and *sarod*, wind instruments such as the transverse bamboo flute and *nagaswaram* (a double-reed pipe that is reminiscent of a saxophone in sound), and drums including sets of *tablas* and the barrel-shaped double-headed *mridangam*. Most have themselves been trained within certain schools of technique and repertoire, and approach the teacher-student relationship with great commitment and seriousness. Music teachers often become a mentor and nearly foster parent to their students, in some cases taking on full direction for the student's overall education, while the students care for the practical needs of the teacher and their household. Indian families who have relocated to other countries, such as the United States, are sometimes able to find a master musician or dancer devotedly teaching students during intense evening or weekend sessions. Many young people in the United States work for years with their teacher and then give a public performance that reveals their mastery of the dance and musical forms, as well as their continued commitment to their heritage.

A tambura

ꙮ All about
Dahee Maatyaar

A Pot of Yogurt

"**D**ahee Maatyaar" is a simple dance-song sung by the Konkani-speaking people of the Saraswat Brahmin sub-caste. The story of Krishna breaking the pot carried by the beautiful girl to get to his favorite food, yogurt, is a common theme of folk dances, as well as classical dance forms such as Kathak, Bharata Natyam, and Manpuri, each having their own stylistic, rhythmic and movement vocabulary. As they sing, young Indian children swing gently, and may alternately step on their right and then their left foot, while holding an imaginary pot on their head.

Lyrics:
Dahee maatyaar ghe-vu-nee Soondari (2x)
Vikku gelyaa Mathuraa Nagari
Vaataith bhetloe Krishnu bhetaloe (2x)
Taaney magull mataka bhetaloe

Translation:
Carrying (a pot of) yogurt on her head, the beautiful one
Goes to the market in the city of Mathura
On the way she meets naughty Krishna
Who breaks the pot of yogurt

ꙮ Extensions

1. Gently sway from left to right, once per measure while singing or playing the song.

2. Krishna is the principal character of many Indian legends and folktales. The great Indian tale, Ramayana, is the story of Krishna's life as an adult named Rama, for which music, dance, theatre, and puppetry performances have been created. Artistic renderings of Krishna appear in many resources including Stuart Welch's book, *Indian Art and Culture, 1300-1900.*

3. While singing, place hands on head as if to steady a clay pot of yogurt. Step to the pulse, first the left and then the right foot, in place. Eventually, children can make their own individual pathways to the "marketplace" while stepping to the song's pulse.

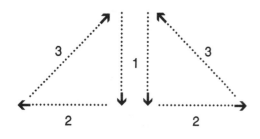

4. Conduct the strong three-beat meter, making large triangles in the air as you sing. (See diagram at left.)

Dahee Maatyaar

(A Pot of Yogurt)

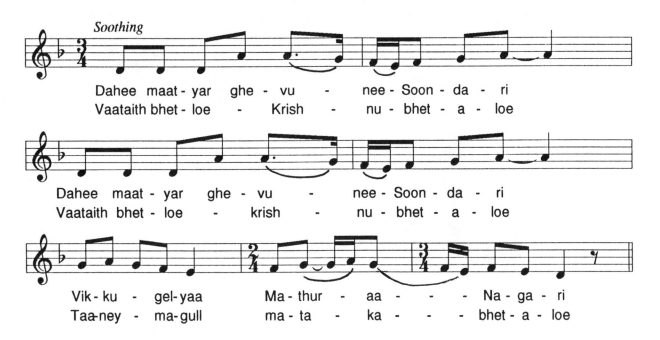

Dahee maat - yar ghe - vu - nee - Soon - da - ri
Vaataith bhet - loe - Krish - nu - bhet - a - loe

Dahee maat - yar ghe - vu - nee - Soon - da - ri
Vaataith bhet - loe - krish - nu - bhet - a - loe

Vik - ku - gel-yaa   Ma - thur - aa - - - Na - ga - ri
Taa-ney - ma-gull   ma - ta - ka - - bhet - a - loe

ʚAll about
Baariye Bubly

Bubly and The Monkey

"**B**aariye Bubly" is a story song about a little girl named Bubly and a monkey which can be accompanied by appropriate actions for the text. It combines Gujarati, the language of a state north of Bombay, with the Hindi language. Interestingly, parts of the song are sung while others are chanted in a rhythmic manner that includes the expressive rising and falling of speech inflections.

Lyrics and gestures:
(Sing): Baariye Bubly baitee thee, baitee thee
Hastee kelaa khaatee thee, khaatee thee
(Bubly sits, eating a banana)

(Chant): Baaharey vaanro baitoe tho,
Baitoe, baitoe, jotoe tho
(Monkey circles eyes with thumb and forefinger, watching Bubly)

(Sing): Vaanar-bhai rey andar aayaa re andar aayaa
Lai kelaa ni bhaagi gayaa, re bhaagi gayaa
(Monkey grabs the banana from Bubly)

(Chant): Bubly-bai na ghbraya gayaa,
Na radiyaa, ni khabray khadaa
(Bubly shakes her head, rubs her eyes in a gesture meaning "No, I will not cry")

(Chant): Gaynd lido, cchhutto phenko,
Pathar lido, cchhutto phenko
(Bubly throws imaginary stone and ball to ground)

(Sing): Vaanar-bhai rey ghabraay gayaa, re bhabraay gayaa
Phenkey kela bhaagee gayaa, re bhaagee gayaa
(Monkey drops the banana and runs)

Translation:
In the window, Bubly sat, Bubly sat,
Smilingly eating a banana, eating a banana.

Outside a monkey was waiting, he was waiting.
He was watching, he was watching.

Brother monkey leaped inside, he leaped inside.
He grabbed the banana and ran away, he ran away.

Little Bubly was not scared at all.
She did not cry. She sat where she was.

She grabbed a stone and threw it down.
She grabbed a ball and threw it down.

Brother Monkey got a fright.
He dropped the banana and ran away.

❧ Extensions

1. Tell the story of Bubly and the monkey in English, chanting rhythmically, adding appropriate gestures and actions. Have children imitate or create gestures using the description as a guide.

2. Listening to the tape, it is easy to hear the differences between sung and chanted, or spoken, parts. Note the repeated phrases of the text and melody, at the ends of the phrases, and also the rhyming words.

3. Enact the song while singing it, either with the group as a whole, or with selected smaller groups learning just two lines apiece. The groups might create descriptive gestures related to their singing or chanting that can be done in place (or, select two children to actively dramatize the actions of Bubly and the monkey).

Baariye Bubly
(Bubly and The Monkey)

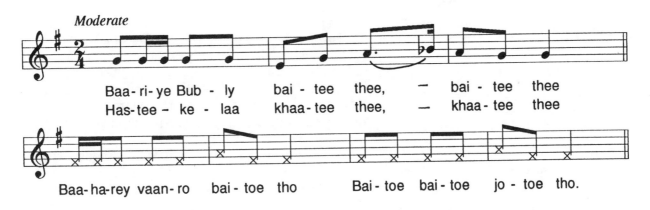

Baa-ri-ye Bub-ly   bai-tee   thee,   —   bai-tee   thee
Has-tee – ke – laa   khaa-tee   thee,   —   khaa-tee   thee

Baa-ha-rey vaan-ro   bai-toe tho   Bai-toe bai-toe jo-toe tho.

Japan

Mayumi Adachi as a young girl.

*"During the summer vacation,
our cousins came
from crowded Tokyo to visit us.
They loved coming because we took
them swimming in the sea
or hiking in the mountains.
Some were very musical,
and we made up songs and stories,
and shared variations
of our favorite game songs.
I always cried
when they went back to Tokyo."*

- Mayumi Adachi

Mayumi Adachi was born in 1961 in the city of Kashiwazaki, in Nigata prefecture. This small western Japanese community is only a two-and-a-half hour ride from downtown Tokyo on a swift "bullet" train. Her father, Eiichiro, ran a liquor shop that was more like a small grocery store that took up one-third of the first floor of their house. Her mother, Mikiko, helped out in the busy store. The remaining two-thirds of the first floor housed the kitchen, family room and bedroom, and upstairs were more bedrooms and a bathroom. Other relatives including her great grandmother, shared the house, and many also lived nearby. Her older brother, Toshikazu, and sister, Naomi, spent lots of time with her, sharing songs and games, and showing her what they had learned in school music classes, at the playground, and during their organ lessons. She loved it all. She heard traditional Japanese music on visits to Shinto shrines, and once in a while at school. Her fourth grade music teacher played *koto*, the long zither played with three ivory picks. Mayumi and her classmates were allowed to try the instrument on a visit to the teacher's home.

Towards the end of each year in December, just before New Year's, the family exchanged gifts. Her family, being Buddhist and Shinto, did not celebrate Christmas, but they celebrated friendship and family at about the same time of the year. Her interest in music was strong from an early age, and friends and family knew her favorite gifts were records.

Another enjoyable celebration was in August, when everyone in the community took part in the Bon Odori harvest festival. Mayumi dressed in her *yukata*—the traditional light *kimono*, and wore her special wooden platform sandals called *geta*. Friends and family went together to the yards of the Shinto shrines, or an open space, and danced in a circle around the taiko drummers performing on a raised stand constructed for the occasion, or to recorded music. Old and young danced together informally. School children learned particular Bon Odori dances to perform at the end of the annual school sports festivals and used those dances during the August Bon Odori festival.

In 1985 Mayumi arrived in New York to study the Robert Pace piano instruction method, and received her master's degree at Teacher's College of Columbia University. She is a doctoral candidate in music at the University of Washington.

40

Slightly smaller than California but with a population of 117 million, Japan is a country made up of four large islands (Hokkaido, Honshu, Shikoku and Kyushu) and many smaller ones. Situated east of Korea and northeast of China, much of its terrain is mountainous with several active and nonactive volcanoes soaring straight up from towns nestled at their feet. Never more than fifty miles from the ocean, the rugged mountains contrast with miles of seacoast. This dramatic landscape is a palpable presence in Japan, the inspiration of poets, artists and musicians.

Although Hokkaido, the northernmost island has long snowy winters similar to Maine, the rest of the country copes with a climate similar to the southern states. Winter is cold and wet, sometimes snowy, and the summer is hot and humid with torrential rains in early fall. Intense green is the predominant color of the countryside, as hillside forests contrast with flat rice paddies. The flowering beauty of spring is marked with cultural festivals as the cherry blossoms open, and the rich abundance of fall is celebrated at rice harvest time. Many Japanese ride bikes for transportation, especially students, who might have as much as a 30-minute ride to and from school each day. Families enjoy short trips to Buddhist temples and Shinto shrines, hot springs, and recreations of ancient villages and workshops. Little paper tags with handwritten prayers or wishes flutter in the entries and on trees at the shrines, and tourists may try their hand in making pottery, indigo-dyed cloth, special candles and rice paper at the workshops.

Tokyo, Kyoto, Nara, and Osaka, cities of great historical, cultural, economic, and political significance are located on the central island of Honshu. Honshu is the thriving center of production for cars, cameras and computers which occupy a formidable place in today's international marketplace.

Even today, as a world economic leader, Japan still bows in respect to the ancestors. Medieval emperors, courtiers and samurai warriors are remembered with pride. The merchant and military fleets that later sailed throughout Asia inspire modern businesspeople.

This respect for the past has led Japan into a living preservation of traditional practices. From Japan's cultural treasure chest comes *Chan-no-yu*, the tea ceremony exquisite in its studied simplicity. Comprised of a strict set of movements and gestures for preparing and serving the tea, the ceremony promotes rich enjoyment and complete involvement in the moment. Another ancient form is theater, both the *Kabuki* theater which incorporates dance, music, mime and naturalism and includes symbolic makeup colors and many costume changes, and the *No* drama that uses an all-male cast in elaborate, stylized costumes and makeup and frequently depicts warriors, spirits and demons. In the Kabuki theater, the audience sits on the wooden floor in boxed-off sections for each family or party.

Creative beauty flowing from strict adherence to a particular order is as much in evidence in *Ike bana*, the art of formal flower arrangement as it is in *Origami*, the art of folding paper. The subtlety of a floral composition or the cunning of an origami animal give testimony to the years spent in gaining mastery.

Japanese calligraphy and painting on absorbent rice paper has been practiced for centuries. The Chinese characters called *kanji* are written in broad strokes produced by slow and graceful manipulation of the brush. Students study calligraphy in school as part of the curriculum. Once the forms have been mastered, and after years of patient and meditative practice, a spontaneity is released that is often breathtaking.

Western-style classical, rock and pop music (including all-Japanese bluegrass and salsa bands) are enjoyed by the Japanese as much as their distinctive traditional singers and instrumentalists. Popular at the *matsuri* summer festivals are the athletic masters of the thundering *kodo* and *taiko* drums. The *koto*, a thirteen-stringed floor zither, is perhaps the best known Japanese traditional instrument. The *shamisen*, a three-string plucked lute somewhat like a banjo, is played solo, in small chamber groups, and in *kabuki* and *bunraku* puppet theatre ensembles. Bon Odori, an August festival that brings people home to be with their families, is a good time to hear traditional music at Shinto shrines and in the vicinity of the street vendors who sell traditional food, toys, and crafts while costumed dancers move through the streets. These festivals are opportunities for people to wear traditional clothing, putting aside western-style contemporary Japanese apparel.

All about
Zui Zui Zukkorobashi

Soy Bean Paste

"Zui Zui Zukkorobashi" is a children's singing game that may have originated in Kyoto in this version. At one time there, at harvest time, the new tea leaves were brought in a *chatsubo* (straw-weave basket) to the lord or master. Those bearing the tea went, in procession, through the village to the home of their master. People along the way sat formally, and bowed as the parade passed by. Children found the parade very long and perhaps boring, and devised this counting-out song to amuse themselves. The singing game is played yet today throughout Japan. Mayumi remembers playing this game when the cold winter snows fell in Nigata and children had to play inside a good deal. Twenty or thirty years ago Japanese houses did not have central heating, and so each room had a special table called *kotatsu*, with an electric, gas or charcoal heater under it. All would sit with legs under the table and a blanket or comforter draped over their laps to trap the heat, and play games, read, or talk.

Lyrics:
Zui zui zukkorobashi, gomamiso zui
Chatsubo no oware te toppin-syan,
Nuketara don doko syo.
Tawara no nezumi ga kome kute chu. Chu, chu, chu.
Otto-san ga yonde mo okka-san ga yonde mo.
Ikikko nashi yo.
Ido no mawari de ochawan kaita no dare?

Translation:
Soy bean paste (for making soup)
Take tea leaves in a *chatsubo* bowl (to the master).
When the parade begins,
    run to a friend's house and shut the sliding door.
When the parade passes, let's play outside again.
Mice are in the rice case eating rice,
    squeaking "chu chu chu."
Even if your father or mother call you,
Don't leave us (stay and play).
Who broke the rice bowl around the well?

✺ Extensions

1. Repeat and translate the Japanese words and phrases:
Miso - soy bean paste
Cha - tea
Otto-san - Father or Daddy
Okka-san - Mother or Mommy
Ikikko nashi yo - don't leave us, stay and play
Imagine the sound of a wood-and-paper door sliding closed (*toppin-syan*), and the sound of mice squeaking (*chu chu chu*).

2. Pat the long-short (♪. ♪) rhythm alternating right and left hands on legs.

3. What do the children in the group do to pass the time during foul weather? How are their homes heated?

42

Zui Zui Zukkorbashi

(Soy Bean Paste)

How to Play The Game

• Children gather in small circles of three or four.

• They form their hands into loose fists, in the shape of two small cups or *tawaras* (rice cases) with open lids. (Their thumbs create the lids.)

• A leader points to one *tawara* for each pulse, tapping the index finger on one fist per pulse, while children sing the song.

• The last person tapped at the sound of "re" is expected to "do something," such as to sing a solo, to tell a joke, or to eat a snack, or has to take that hand out of the game.

• The game then starts again, until gradually everyone has removed hands from the circle but one person who is left with one or two hands still in. That person is the "winner."

⌐All about
Kaera No Uta

Frog Song

"**K**aeru No Uta" is a staple of beginning piano books and schoolchildren's songbooks. It is well-known by young Japanese children, who enjoy singing the onomatopoeia of the frog's *gwa* sound. When Mayumi was a child she had small caged birds called *buncho* for pets, then a parakeet that could mimic simple Japanese words. The parakeet's name was Rin-rin, the sound of a bell. All cultures have words that sound like what they are describing.

Lyrics:
Kaeru no uta ga
Kikoete kuruyo:
Gwa gwa gwa gwa
Gero gero gero gero gwa gwa gwa.

Translation:
The song of the frog
I can hear:
Gwa gwa gwa gwa
Gero gero gero gero gwa gwa gwa.

✺ Extensions

1. Sing or play the song. Have the children guess what animal is making the *gwa* sound. Share meaning of *uta* (song), and *kaeru* (frog). Ask children to imitate the sound of a frog, and share with them the rendition of Japanese children. If your community has more than one language spoken, explore with the children how animals "speak" in those languages.

2. Sing the song. Older children may wish to attempt singing the melody in canon, with the second group beginning as the first (leader) group reaches the third measure.

3. Add the sound of wood blocks in a simple ostinato

$$(\; \flat \; \bullet \; \bullet \;)$$

and bells (or triangles) on the first and third beats of each measure.

4. The evolution of folk songs is always fascinating. "Kaeru no Uta" is actually a German folk song! It was translated into Japanese by Toshiaki Okamoto, a former professor of music at Kunitachi Music College, and published a century ago in Japanese song books. When Hokkaido Broadcast Company of Japan researched the origins of the song in Berlin in 1994, they were dismayed to find out that no one knew the melody— despite its supposed origin there! Create an English-language version with your group as a springboard to explore "the folk process."

Kaeru No Uta

(Frog Song)

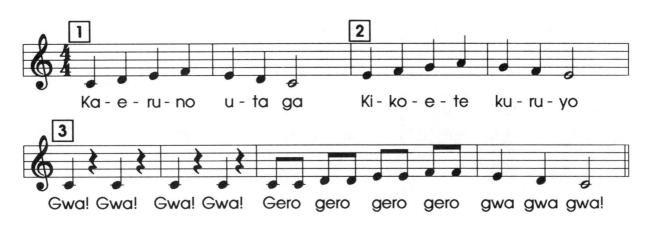

Ka - e - ru - no   u - ta ga   Ki - ko - e - te   ku - ru - yo

Gwa! Gwa!   Gwa! Gwa!   Gero gero   gero gero   gwa gwa gwa!

Korea

Alice Kim as a child, in traditional dress

Alice Kim came with her family to the United States in 1982, influenced by the promise of a good life and jobs for all. The one-year ESL (English as a second language) course she enrolled in soon after her arrival accelerated her adjustment to American life. She completed high school and went on to major in music at the University of Washington.

Alice began to study piano at age seven, in Korea. Her family was a singing family. They enjoyed singing lullabies, children's songs, holiday songs, and popular pieces learned from TV and radio. She carried her love of music with her to the United States and is currently completing her training as a music teacher. Alice remembers singing "Ha'kyo Jung," possibly Korea's most famous children's song, with her mother and father. She played "Achim Baram," a singing game, first with her parents, sister and cousins and later on with girlfriends at school.

"I remember singing a lot at home and in school while growing up in Korea. Even on the very first day of my school career, we learned a song from our first grade teacher, with movements to go with it. I can still hear it, and I sing it even today."

- Alice Kim

Koreans constitute one of the largest communities of Asian people currently living in the United States. Coming primarily from South Korea, they have settled especially in New York City, Los Angeles and the Seattle-Tacoma area.

A nation for over 2,000 years, Korea means "Land of Morning Calm." South Korea is part of a peninsula about the size of Minnesota, separated from China by the Yellow Sea and from Japan by the Sea of Japan. Conquered first by one and then the other of these two powerful neighbors, Korea achieved independence following defeat of the Japanese in 1948 and was divided into North (Democratic People's Republic of Korea) and South (Republic of Korea) Korea, at the 38th latitudinal parallel. This dividing line was maintained after the Korean War of 1950-53 which involved North and South Korea, the United States, U.N. forces and China.

Historically, Korea managed to resist foreign domination and maintain its own independent kingdoms for several centuries. During this time a language distinctive both in sound and script developed. Even under Chinese and Japanese rule, Koreans maintained their own unique culture. Korean cuisine and etiquette are easily distinguished from

46

those of neighboring East Asian countries as are its traditional clothing and music. Confucianism and Buddhism are both practiced today along with Chondogyo, the "religion of the heavenly way" a faith indigenous to Korea.

Today South Korea is a technologized world power, an economically stable country keeping pace with other East Asian giants.

The *kayakeum* and *komungo*, long floor zithers with twelve and five strings respectively, are indigenous musical instruments of Korea. Their distinctive percussive sounds are produced by snapping the strings against the thin body of the instruments. The ethereal, "other worldly" sound of the *chongak* or *aak* music of the royal court ensemble, with its drums, gongs, reed and string instruments, preserve traditions that date back to the fifth or sixth century. Considered "museum music," *chongak* is rarely performed today. On the other hand, the folk songs of the fisherman and farmers are still sung in rural areas.

When Korea opened its doors to the West in the middle of the nineteenth century, all manner of new influences flooded in. By 1900, the Yi dynasty had replaced the traditional court orchestra with a Western-style military band. Nothing remained untouched. In less than a century, Korean taste in music and education was thoroughly westernized.

Concerts and recitals of Western classical music are popular, and many Koreans study piano or violin. Like young people everywhere, Korean teenagers listen to American and European, as well as Korean, Japanese, and Chinese rock and pop musicians.

Nonetheless, Korean parents and grandparents still sing the old songs to their children, and teachers still offer them the gift of their musical heritage in school.

Traditional music can be heard at New Year's festivities, which Koreans celebrate both on January 1 and sometime in February, when the traditional lunar new year occurs.

Another festive Korean holiday takes place in June. "Tano" is Korea's spring festival, which began in ancient times as a planting ceremony. Children love Tano, which is celebrated with wrestling matches and swinging competitions. Many towns erect very tall swings in advance of the day so that the children may practice swinging as high as possible. In the competitions, the children must hit bells with their foot while they are airborne on their swing. The child who rings the bell the most times is the winner. At one time people may have believed that swinging high would encourage the crops planted at this time to grow high, emulating the children on the swings.

The traditional Korean house was built around an enclosed courtyard. Unlike westerners who closed their doors and windows when talking about a private matter, Asian people opened their doors when they wanted to keep a secret. This is because in a traditional house the doors and windows were fitted with a strong, thick paper which let air and light in. Of course it let sound in and out freely as well, so people opened their doors when speaking confidentially, so no one could hide in the shadow of a closed door eavesdropping. The floors were covered with a special oiled paper. To keep from ripping this paper, people left their shoes outside the house on a narrow rack known as a *"maru."* The homes were heated by flues which ran under the floor and carried the warm air from the kitchen stoves back to the rest of the house.

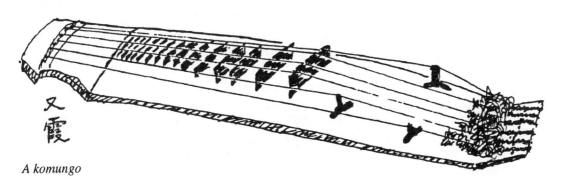

A komungo

~All about
Ha'kyo Jung

The School Bell is Ringing

In anticipation of attending school, "Ha'kyo Jung" is sung by children from three years onward through the primary grades. Composed by Mary Kimm Joh in the early 1940s, it is so well known in Korea and in Korean communities in other countries that many think of it as an ancient folk song. (Mary Kimm Joh is now 90, and lives in New York City.) The deeper meaning of this song is the implied respect that all Korean students have for their teachers. The school bell is ringing! Hurry up! Don't keep the teacher waiting for us! Be sure to work together today as always to maintain harmony in the class, pay attention to your studies and do well. In a Korean children's schoolbook, this song was published using pictures of bells instead of music notes on a large staff!

Lyrics: (Transliteration of Korean characters)
Ha'kyo jung ee: daeng daeng (daeng) (or use *tchin'da*)
Uhza mo ee jha
Sun saeng nim ee oo ree rul,
Kida ree shin da.

(A second verse changes lines 3 & 4 to:
Sa ee joht keh oh nuhldoh, Khong bu jhal ha jha.)

Translation:
The school bell is ringing: tang tang tang (ring it!).
Let's hurry up, gather around and meet.
There waiting for us is
Teacher. (*shin da* is a term of respect for an older person).
(Verse 2, lines 3 and 4: Getting along peacefully, today as always.
Study, do well.)

∾ Extensions

1. The words "tchin' da" indicate the action of ringing the bell; some of the singers can mime pulling in rhythm on that old-fashioned bell rope.

2. Discuss the text. Teach children to speak the first and last phrases: "Ha'kyo jung ee" and "Kida ree shin da." Is the "daeng" of the Korean school bell a sound they hear in their own lives? (Don't pronounce the *ng* too strongly.)What words in English describe the sound of a bell? (brrring, ring, ding-dong) Note the similar "ng" ending on the Korean and English words.

3. Sing the song, adding these rhythmic movements: pat the pulse, then clap the running eighth notes, pat the walking quarter notes on the lap, and stamp on the slower half notes. Later, add a wood block, drums, and gongs, respectively, to the durational values, or to accentuate certain notes or words.

Ha'kyo Jung
(The School Bell Is Ringing)

Ha' - kyo jung ee daeng daeng daeng, Uh - za mo ee jha,

Sun saeng nim ee oo ree rul, ki - da ree shin da.

~All about
Achim Baram

Cold Morning Wind

"**A**chim Baram" is a singing game whose ritualistic playing-out of the rules nurtures a child's need for structure, even in play. "Scissors-Rock-Paper" is played by children in many cultures, although generally without an associated song. Two children face each other as they sing, hand-clapping some sections and miming other parts of the text. The text jumps from seagulls to teachers writing postcards, but this inconsistency seems not to matter to children who enjoy the sound, the movement, and the game.

Lyrics (transliteration) and movements:
Sei, sei, sei.
(Partners hold hands, bouncing them up and down)
Achim baram chan baram ae
(Clap own hands, cross to clap partner's hands; repeat.)
Ulgo ganun jau girogi
(Wipe left and right eyes, pretending to cry. Point to imaginary flying seagull, left and right)
Uri sungseng gye shil jogae
(Cross chest, first with right and then left hand. Nod head right, then left)
Yupso hanjang so juseyo
(Act out writing postcard on the hand)
Hanjang malgo doo jang iyo
(Brush own hands vertically 8X, as if to say "Now the task is done.")
Goori, goori, goori, goori
(Roll hands in circles around each other)
Gawee bawee bo!
(On "bo", extend hand in one of three ways:
Index and middle fingers in scissors shape
Fist for rock
Flat for paper)

Translation:
(Sei, Sei, Sei is not translatable, but functions as a rhythmic introduction.)
Cold morning wind.
Seagull crying in the morning.
While our teachers are staying here,
Write him/her a postcard.
Not one but two postcards.
Rolling, rolling, rolling, rolling.
Rock, scissors, paper.

❧ Extensions

1. Repeat the words "Gawee bawee bo," shaping hands for scissors, rock, or paper on the word *bo*.
Roll the hands in circles around each other while reciting *goori*. Explain that *goori* probably comes from *goo ruda*, a verb meaning "to roll."
Practice with partners.

2. Explain the game. Scissors wins over paper because scissors cuts paper. Paper wins over rock because paper covers rock. Rock wins over scissors because rock crushes scissors. In Korea the loser bends his/her head forward and the winner taps the loser's neck with a finger. The winner then opens a hand to show five separate fingers, and the loser must guess which finger tapped him. While playing the game, children sometimes choose the same element (scissors, rock, paper). This tie is broken by doing the "gawee bawee bo" chant over again.

3. Sing or play the song and demonstrate the motions. Each singing, clapping and acting-out phrase is eight pulses.

Achim Baram
(*Cold Morning Wind*)

Sei, sei, sei.

A - chim ba - ram chan ba-ram ae
Ul - go ga - nun jau gi-ro - gi
U - ri sung - seng gye shil jo-gae
Yup - so han - jang so ju-se-yo
Hah - jang mal - go doo jang-i - yo

Goo - ri, goo - ri, goo - ri, goo - ri Ga-wee ba-wee bo!

Jerry Teik-Chaun at the piano

*"Children in Malaysia like to sing.
Kindergarten children think
that's what school is all about:
singing.
I remember
that our school days began
with singing for nearly an hour.
And then we would scamper
around the room while the teacher
played the piano.
Most of the teachers played piano
well enough for movement."*

- Jerry Teik-Chuan Lim

Malaysia

Jerry Teik-Chuan Lim was born in Pulau Pinang, an island-state on the west coast of Malaysia. He spoke Fukien-Chinese at home, and is the fifth generation of a family that journeyed far from their homeland in southeast China to settle in Malaysia. In school he learned to speak both Malay and English. He began his piano training quite early, passed the British standard exams in music and piano, and came to the United States in 1987 to study at the University of Washington. With a strong interest in both commercial and classical music, he has performed as a keyboard player in Malaysian rock bands. Having received his B.A. in music and education, he is now a master's student in music, majoring in education and technology.

The Malay peninsula stretches from Thailand southward towards Indonesia, with Singapore situated at its southern tip. Historically an important stopping-off point, ships would often drop anchor in the peninsula's archipelago and wait for the monsoon winds to shift before traveling on. This strategic location at the crossroads of an important trade route between India and China led the Malays into significant cultural exchange as early as the seventh century. By the ninth century they were trading with the Arabs. Portugal occupied parts of the peninsula in the sixteenth century and by the late eighteenth century Malaysia was a British colony.

Today Malaysia is a multiethnic nation with a population composed of 55% Malays, 34% Chinese, 10% Indian and Pakistanis, and 1% European, Eurasian, and blended nationalities.

Malaysians are generally bi- or even tri-lingual, speaking Malay and English, as well as their own mother tongue when it differs from Malay. Religions as well as languages coexist harmoniously and include Buddhism, Hinduism, Islam, and Christianity. Schools are organized according to the British system, with instruction presented in English and Malay and British-style examinations given periodically.

Malay, Middle Eastern, Indian, Chinese and Western influences are all reflected in Malaysian music. The strong affinity for Western European culture felt throughout Malaysia extends to the performing arts. Traditional music is still heard however, primarily in the theatre, at puppet shows or as an accompaniment to dance. Muslim, Hindu or animistic ceremonies and rituals also incorporate the older musical forms and instruments.

Drums and gongs are at the heart of Malay instrumental music, and wooden xylophones similar to those of neighboring Indonesia are heard in traditional ensembles. The court's chamber ensemble, *nawbat*, features Islamic-flavored ornamental music on strings and percussion. Indian children take private music lessons and learn to play Karnatic instruments as well as traditional regional songs and dances from the south of India.

Chinese immigrants founded schools that preserve their own culture and music. Religious chanting is heard in their temples, along with slit-drums, gongs and bells. Chinese opera companies offering Cantonese-style opera are popular among the Malaysian Chinese.

The Western impact is still considerable. Many middle-class children take classical piano and violin lessons. American, European, and Malaysian rock music is available in stores and is extremely popular with young people. Interaction of the various cultures has resulted in fusion music such as *ronggeng*, *joget*, and music for quadrille and line dances.

Malaysian actresses of Chinese descent

Těpok Amai-amai

Ladybug

"Těpok amai-amai" is a children's song featuring the Malay language and a European-style diatonic melody. Most children learn the song in kindergarten or first grade. The lyrics address the children as lady-bugs, grasshoppers, and colorful butterflies. The many insects affectionately referred to represent the many nationalities in Malaysia. Coconut milk is a Malaysian sweet, and an important ingredient in curried meat dishes. On the tape, the use of a wooden xylophone to play the melody offers a taste of the indigenous Southeast Asian sound, and the sound of the goblet drum suggests Islamic influence. Malaysian society is patriarchal with the father at the head of the family. The phrase "mother has work to do" refers to work traditionally done by women—caring for children and preparing meals.

Malay Pronunciation

- "k" is silent at the end of a word.

- "ě" and "a" = f*a*r

- "i" = m*ee*t, "o" = g*o*, "u" = b*oo*

Lyrics:
Těpok amai-amai bělalang kupu-kupu
Těpok ramai ramai ěmak upah susu
Susu lěmak manis santan k'lapa muda
Adek jangan m'nangis ěmak ada kerja.

Translation:
Clap little lady-bugs,
grasshoppers and colorful butterflies.
Clap, everyone.
Mother will give you coconut milk, rich and sweet,
the sweetest coconut milk from the young fruits.
Little brother, don't cry.
Mother has work to do.

✣ Extensions

1. Listen for the sound of the xylophone and drum to complement the singing.

2. Try speaking selected Malay words and phrases:
těpok – clap
ěmak – mother
susu – coconut milk
santan – coconut
jangan m'nangis – don't cry

3. Note words referring to Malaysia's lush tropical environment: ladybugs, butterflies, coconuts.

4. Sing the song standing in a circle, then clap and step to the pulse. Move to the right as you sing. As Malaysian teachers do, cue children (visually or with a tap on a drum) to clap twice as fast or twice as slow while singing at the same speed.

Tĕpok Amai-amai

(Ladybug)

Tĕ - pok a - mai a - mai Bĕ - la - lang ku - pu ku - pu Te -

pok ra - mai ra - mai Ĕ - mak u - pah su - su Su -

su lĕ - mak ma - nis san - tan k'la - pa mu - da A -

dek jan - gan m'na - ngis Ĕ - mak a - da kĕr - ja.

Vietnam

Phong Thuyet Nguyen

*"My family,
although musicians,
have long been farmers of rice
and also fruit trees
- orange, tangerine,
banana, mango, and others.
Our fruit orchard stretched
over several acres.
Sometimes
in the afternoon
people of all ages
would get together
in the yard of our brick house
and sing."*

- Phong Thuyet Nguyen

Phong Thuyet Nguyen was raised in Can Tho province in the Mekong delta of South Vietnam, in a village called Tam Ngai. He was born into a very musical family that played many types of music from art music to music for festivals and ceremonies, to theatrical music. When he was very young, his mother sometimes sang to him while she did needlework. At the age of five he began his musical training with his father, concentrating first on singing, then, at the age of ten, adding instrumental instruction. Even as a child he performed in many provinces of South Vietnam.

A familiar scene that Phong recalls fondly are the boats commonly used on rivers in South Vietnam where he lived. One type goes from one city to another—the current flowing boat. On the same body of water is found another kind that takes people from one side of the river to the other—a crossing boat. Many are very long and narrow in design to make it easier to flow quickly along with the current, and they are stretched out so there is plenty of room to carry many things. The river boaters sing to each other and tease each other as they move along with the current. Sometimes they sing songs that test the boater's knowledge, some that talk about the friendships made on the river. Some songs reflect philosophically on where the currents take the boaters.

Over the years Phong specialized in the playing of the *dan tranh* zither, *dan nguyet* lute, and *dan bau* monochord. Eventually, he moved to Saigon, where he studied Western music, and earned a degree in literature and philosophy from the University of Saigon. Then Phong became a teacher of literature and principal of a Saigon high school. In 1970-74 he introduced and taught classes in Vietnamese traditional music, not previously taught in schools. He left Saigon in 1974. Phong received his Ph.D. in ethnomusicology at the Sorbonne University in Paris.

A visiting scholar and performer on the faculties of Kent State University, the University of Pittsburgh, and the University of Washington, he has contributed many recordings, books and articles on Vietnamese and Vietnamese-American music. He now lives and teaches in Ohio and travels often to Vietnam, leading scholarly expeditions to research the traditional performing arts in modern Vietnam.

Vietnam lies south of China, bordered by Cambodia and Laos on the west, and the sea (Gulf of Tonkin, South China, and Gulf of Thailand) on its eastern side. "Two baskets of rice slung on a pole" is a description the Vietnamese offer of their country. The baskets are the deltas of the Red River in the north and the Mekong in the south, and the carrying pole of those rice baskets is a series of mountain chains along the western border, known as the Annamite Cordillera which run almost the entire 1,000 mile length of the country. Monsoon season is June to November, bringing intense heat, typhoons, heavy rains and flooding to the countryside, with the Red and Mekong rivers frequently overflowing their banks. About fifty-nine inches of rain falls in Vietnam, but Hanoi, in the north, receives an incredible seventy-two inches! Houses in the delta areas are raised on poles to minimize the effects of the flooding. Rice thrives in this warm, wet climate. One of the world's leading producers of the grain, Vietnamese farmers cultivate over twelve million acres of rice. Not only a diet staple, rice provides the raw materials for making beer, wine, flour, straw mats, paper, garments, fuel, and fertilizer.

Many varieties of rice and fish form the staple of the Vietnamese diet, and tropical fruits, ginger, mint, sugar cane and herbs are also abundant.

The Vietnamese have maintained their own ethnic and cultural character through the ages, although ouside influences have played a part in shaping this identity. When the country endured ten centuries of Chinese domination, ending in 939 A.D., many of the trappings of this culture were absorbed. Vietnamese philosophy, character script, social customs, and the art of planting rice bear the characteristic stamp of the Mandarin way. Traders and merchants from India journeyed to Vietnam's coastal communities and courts during the country's formative years, where an exchange of beliefs as well as trade goods took place. The nation matured during its Buddhist-influenced Golden Period of Vietnamese Culture, from the tenth through the fourteenth centuries. In the fifteenth century Vietnam scored a decisive victory over Champa (now Southern Vietnam) and grew in area to its present size.

The French established a protectorate in Indochina in 1861 which included Laos, Cambodia, and Vietnam. At this point Vietnam's westernization accelerated rapidly as French-styled schooling and the French language was introduced. A rift between northern communist and southern democratic political ideologies divided the country in 1954. Continued aggression by northerners, led by Ho Chi Minh, led to a disastrous military response by the United States. Following almost ten years of escalation during which many thousands died, a cease fire was signed in 1973. Today Vietnam celebrates its history and traditional culture even as it continues to modernize and stabilize its economy.

Many Vietnamese who sought asylum from the war now live in France, Australia, and the United States. "Little Saigons" (large communities of transplanted Vietnamese) are found in California, Texas, Louisiana and Washington state. Their flight and resettlement, although painful, has offered hope for a renaissance of Vietnamese cultural traditions. It is not unusual to see traditional holidays observed in these communities, including the lunar New Year festival, Tet.

There are many ancient instruments still popular today in Vietnam and also played by students in Vietnamese communities in other parts of the world. Prominent for solo or chamber ensemble use is the *dan bau*, a one-stringed zither, Vietnam's national instrument. The *dan tranh*, a 16- or 17-stringed zither resembling the Chinese *zheng* or Japanese *koto* is often heard as well.

Life in exile and love for their native country are recurrent song themes for Vietnamese living abroad, as are new songs dealing with social, political, and educational matters.

Sophisticated instrumental and theatrical music, as well as children's songs and folk melodies, are often varied and improvised from a skeletal melody. Spoken Vietnamese rises and falls in pitch with a subtlety that lends itself to the creation of highly ornamented music. The work songs of farmers in the rice fields and fishermen on the seacoasts reflect a countryside and way of life in many ways unchanged through several centuries.

Cùm Nụm Cùm Nịu

Close Your Hands

"Cùm Nụm Cùm Nịu" is a counting-out chant sung by children in southern Vietnam. Gathering in small groups, they stack their fists one on top of the other in a long vertical column. A leader taps one fist for each pulse with an index finger. On the last word/beat, the owner of the last fist tapped is "It." The seeker, or "It," covers his/her eyes and counts to ten while the other children run to hiding places. The song contains only four pitches, but many *phonemes*, or Vietnamese language sounds. Phong learned the game from friends when he was five or six. He played it in the front yard of his house, or in the temple yard (frequently used as a gathering spot). The words of the song are not related to each other except by sound—they were put together because of the sound of the rhyme, not because of any particular meaning. They serve to distract everybody, to confuse the fists!

Lyrics and pronunciation:

Cùm nụm cùm nịu, tay tí, tay tiên
(koom noom koom new, tah-ee tee tah-ee tee-en)

Đồng tiền chiếc đũa, hột lúa ba bông
(dong tee-en tsee-ek doo-ah, hoh(t) loo-ah bah boh-ng)

Ăn trộm ăn cắp, trứng gà
(ahng troh-m ahng kahp, trew-ng gah)

Bù xa bù xích
(boo sah boo sik)

Con rắn con rít, thì ra tay nầy.
(korn rahng korn reet, thee rah tah-ee nay-ee)

Translation:
Close your hands! Close your hands!
Pretty hands, fairy's hands.
Golden coins, Chop-stick.
A grain of rice making three flowers.
The thief steals eggs. Beetles and insects.
It's this hand!

Extensions

1. Keep the steady pulse by tapping one closed fist into the palm of the other hand. Change hands for each phrase, when the singers on the recording can be heard taking a breath.

2. Read the English translation, and discuss phrases that refer to Vietnamese culture. For example:
Golden coins are fastened together into jingling percussion instruments.
Like the Chinese, Vietnamese people often eat with long wooden chopsticks.
Rice is the staple food of the Vietnamese.

3. Translate and then chant:
Cùm nụm cùm nịu - close your hands
tay tí, tay tiên - pretty hands, fairy's hands
ra tay nầy - it is this hand

4. Sing the song. Isolate the words for the first line only, and sing "la" on all remaining phrases. Then try to learn lines two, three and four individually, continuing with "la" for remaining lines. With older children, try to sing as many of the Vietnamese words as possible.

5. Play the counting-out game, designating a leader who will count fists, one per pulse. A variation on the game consists of singing the song repeatedly until there is only one fist remaining; that person can choose the next song, game, or activity.

Cùm Nụm Cùm Nịu
(Close Your Hands)

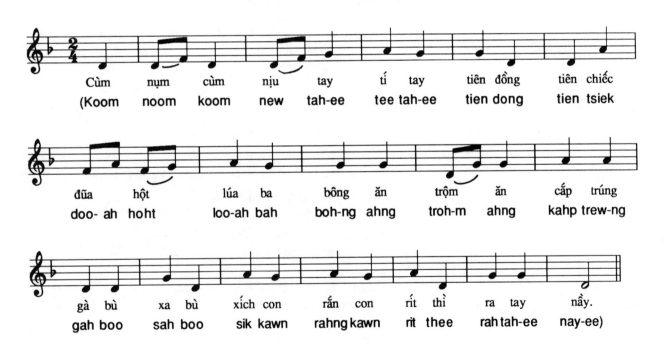

ℒAll about
Qua Cầu Gió Bay

Wind on the Bridge

People all over Saigon sing "Qua Cầu Gió Bay." Live stage performances as well as recorded and broadcast versions popularized the song. It is traditionally sung during spring and autumn festivals centered around the themes of planting and harvesting. During these festivals, groups of young people gather in a house, on a hill, by a lake, in a rice field, or in the Buddhist temple yard. The boys and girls might sing this song in an antiphonal style: the girls will sing a verse, and then the boys will answer with a response to the words, partially improvised on the spot.

The traditional Vietnamese custom of parents arranging their children's marriages is gently challenged through the song's text in which a young man gives generously to his new love. He is willing to "give the shirt off his back," as well as his cone-shaped straw hat and ring to her, all gifts which must be kept secret so as not to displease his mother and father, who might think he is acting improperly by offering such gifts, or being too direct. When questioned by his parents regarding the whereabouts of each of his possessions, he claims that "the wind on the bridge has taken it away."

Today young Vietnamese people, especially those living in communities abroad, have begun to make their own decisions regarding love and marriage. This song expresses the conflicts of living and loving in a time of change, and in the shadow of long-standing tradition. Children in Vietnam enjoy listening to this song, sung by parents and older siblings. The story is sometimes acted out between verses, with the children singing the wind's part in the last phrase as a response.

Lyrics and pronunciation:

1. Yêu nhau cởi (áo) ý a cho nhau. (2.nón; 3.nhẫn)
(Ee-ew nya-oo ker-ee ao ee ah tsaw nya-oo.)

Về nhà dối rằng cha dối mẹ a ý a.
(Vay nyah zoh-ee zang tsah zoh-ee mae ah ee ah.)

Rằng a ý a qua cầu. Rằng a ý a qua cầu.
(Zang ah ee ah kwa ka-oo.)

Chorus: Tình tình tình gió bay. (2x)
(Ting ting ting zaw bay-ee.)

Final Chorus: Tình tình tình gió bay.
(Ting ting ting zaw bay-ee.)

Tình tình tình dánh rơi.
(Ting ting ting dah-n zer-ee.)

Translation:
Loving you I give you my shirt. (hat, ring)
Coming back home, I tell my father and mother:
On the bridge, the wind has taken it away.
(Last verse: On the bridge, because of the wind, it has dropped into the river.)

✢ Extensions

1. Tell the story of the young man who, on each of three days, leaves home with a shirt, hat, or ring, and comes home without it, and that he gives his possessions to a loved one, but tells his parents the wind on the bridge have taken them. Have you ever given something to a special friend, something that was so valuable your parents might be upset if they knew?

2. Sing softly the sound of the wind: *Tình tình tình gió bay.* In keeping with the smaller vocal range of young children, the "tinh" can be sung on "e," the first line of the staff.

3. Sing or play the recording, pantomiming the items as they are given away. The children may sing the young man's response, and/or the chorus—the sound of the wind.

Qua Cầu Gió Bay
(Wind on the Bridge)

1. Yêu nhau cởi - áo ý a cho nhau. - - Về -
(Ee-ew nya-oo ker- ee ao ee ah tsaw nya- oo Vay

nhà dối - rằng cha dối - mẹ a - ý - a Rằng
nyah zoh- ee zang tsah zoh- ee mae ah ee ah Zang

Chorus:

a ý - a - qua - cầu Rằng a ý - a - qua - cầu. Tình
ah ee ah kwa kah-oo Zang ah ee ah kwa ka-oo Ting

tình tình gió - - - bay Tình tình tình gió - - - bay.
ting ting zaw - - - bay-ee Ting ting ting zaw - - - bay-ee)

The Caribbean

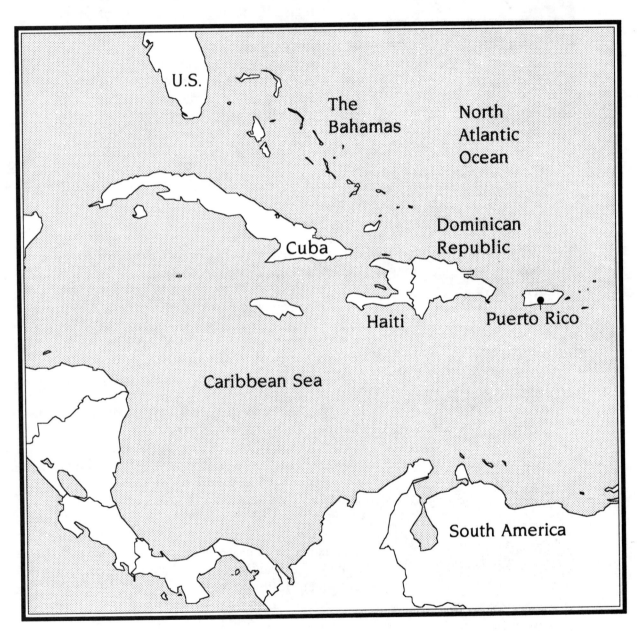

U.S.

The
Bahamas

North
Atlantic
Ocean

Cuba

Dominican
Republic

Haiti

Puerto Rico

Caribbean Sea

South America

Puerto Rico

Puerto Rico

Ricardo as a young boy

*"I come from a large
musical family.
Every time we got together
at my grandfather's house,
the whole family celebrated by
singing, playing, and dancing.
My grandfather and uncle,
musicians in the Symphony
Orchestra of Puerto Rico,
would bring out their violins.
And when the children
sang their songs and danced
we would all join in,
singing and clapping."*

—Ricardo Morla Rios

Ricardo Morla Rios was born in Santurce, a town across the bridge from San Juan, Puerto Rico's capital city. His paternal great-grandfather, Ramon Morla, was a well known composer, and organist at the Cathedral of San Juan. Rafael Rios Rey, his maternal grandfather is a muralist of great renown, whose paintings are displayed on the walls of hotels, city buildings, and mausoleums.

Encouraged by his parents to study piano from an early age, Ricardo's persistence paid off when he was awarded a scholarship to study at the Aspen Music Festival. He continued his studies in Los Angeles. After four years of service in the U.S. Navy, he resumed his study of music and education at the University of Washington. When he isn't performing Bach or Chopin, Ricardo leads a popular Latin dance band, *Calor Tropical*.

Puerto Rico is one of the larger islands in the Caribbean Sea, located centrally among the islands of the West Indies. It lies south of Miami, Florida, east of Mexico and Central America, and north of Colombia and Venezuela. Smooth white sand beaches quickly give way to steep mountains that are dotted with cottages surrounded by banana and plantain trees and small agricultural plots. The tropical rain forest, El Yunque, is home to many species of birds, lizards, the little tree frogs known as *coqui*, and great varieties of enormous plants. Acres of sugar cane create a green blanket for the valleys. Heavy trucks, carrying the harvested cane to the facilities where it will be made into sugar and molasses, careen along steep, twisting mountain roads at breakneck speed, loudly honking a warning to cars unfortunate enough to be in their path.

Columbus landed on the island in 1493, finding the Arawak people, a peaceful group who fished and farmed. The Spanish explorer Juan Ponce de León followed in 1508 and founded gold mining and agricultural ventures that proved unsuccessful over time. Puerto Rico's strategic location seemed of greater interest to the countries that tried to wrest it from Spanish control, including France, England and Holland. It was attacked so often that fortified walls were raised to defend the area around San Juan.

More ingredients were added to Puerto Rico's ethnic potpourri when African slaves were imported to work the sugar cane plantations in the late sixteenth century, but it wasn't until the nineteenth century that Puerto Rico developed into a plantation economy based on sugar, coffee and tobacco. Following the Spanish American War of 1898, Puerto Rico ended its cultural exchange of over 400 years with Spain and entered a voluntary economic and political bond with the United States. Puerto Rico's status as a commonwealth of the United States is now the topic of heated debate. Some feel that Puerto Rico should become the 51st state, others favor complete independence for the island, and others would like to continue its commonwealth status. Although their local government enjoys complete autonomy, the people of Puerto Rico are United States citizens and have no restrictions on immigration. Children attending school in Puerto Rico learn to read English even as they continue to speak Spanish, and become acquainted with North American culture through TV, films, videos, pop songs on the radio, contact with tourists and by visits from relatives living on the mainland.

The economic depression of the 1930s brought the first wave of Puerto Rican immigrants seeking farm and factory jobs to the United States. Today there are more Puerto Ricans living in New York City than there are in Puerto Rico. (They are sometimes called Newyoricans.) The entire community turns out yearly for an enormous fiesta-like parade that celebrates Puerto Rican heritage, in the first week of June.

The vibrant rhythms of Caribbean music reverberate around the world, possibly the region's largest export! Musical genres of Hispanic origin, such as the *seis* and *aguinaldo*, use both the Spanish guitar and the *cuatro* (a small guitar with five doubled strings, considered the national instrument of Puerto Rico). Song styles that often narrate contemporary events or viewpoints, developed into dance music. Exhibiting a strong African influence, Puerto Rican pop music often features traditional drums such as congas, bongos and timbales, and just as often now includes keyboard and brasses. Indigenous instruments are also prominent, including the *guiro* (dried, hollowed gourds of varying sizes, with ridges that are scraped rhythmically using a sort of comb, *maracas* (a pairs of hollowed dried gourds filled with seeds or pebbles), and *claves* (a pair of thick, resonant hardwood sticks struck together in set patterns that provide the rhythmic foundation and feeling for a piece).

Although Puerto Rico's indigenous people, the Arawak and Tainos Indians, had largely disappeared by the late sixteenth century, there is now a movement among some Puerto Ricans to research and reclaim their indigenous heritage. The *jíbaro* people, living simply in rustic surroundings in the mountains, are seen by many as carriers of some of the oldest traditions unchanged for generations, including music, customs and folklore. It is not unusual for young adults in search of their roots to seek out the *jíbaro* as a living cultural archive.

The threads of multiple cultures are woven together to form the modern *Puertorriqueños*—the evidence is clearly seen in many shades of skin color (even within the same family), varieties of facial features, music, dance, instruments, celebrations, and food. The prevailing attitude toward this blending is summed up in the Puerto Rican expression, embraced by Caribbean people in general: "We people are all the colors of the rainbow. We are mixed and blended."

∽ All about
Cheki Morena

Shake it!

"Cheki Morena" is a popular singing game learned by children when they are four or five years old and played throughout the primary grades. It is reminiscent of the African-American game song "Shake it Baby, Shake it," and might have been adapted from that game by Puerto Ricans living in New York in the same neighborhoods as African-Americans. (The word "cheki" is probably a Spanish pronunciation of "shake it," with no Spanish verb related to it.)

Lyrics:
Cheki, morena, cheki
Cheki, morena, !jue!
¿Que a donde esta ese
Ritmo caramba
Del merecumbe?

Un pasito alante
Y otro para atrás
Y dando la vuelta
Y dando la veulta
¿Quien se quedara?

Translation:
Shake it, brown girl, shake it,
Shake it, brown girl, hey!
Where's (meaning, show us) that
flashy (wild, exciting, WOW!) rhythm
of the *merecumbe* (a popular dance).

One small step forward
And another small step step back.
Going round in a circle
Going round in a circle
Who will be the next?

❧ Extensions

1. Note the syncopated rhythm of the words *cheki morena*

♪♩ ♪♩♩

Chant and pat this typical rhythm on your laps. The bongo rhythm heard on the recording is also syncopated, common to Caribbean/Puerto Rican music.

2. Learn the phrases in Spanish:
!Jue! - a joyfully expressed "hey"
¡Ay, Caramba - Good heavens, good gracious, wow!
¿Que a donde esta ese ritmo? - Where is that rhythm?
Dando la vuelta - Going around.
¿Quien se quedara - Who will be the next?
Trigueña is coffee or olive-colored skin
morena is darker brown. These references are commonly found in Puerto Rican songs, and are not slurs, simply fondly descriptive.

Cheki, Morena

(Shake It!)

18

Che-ki mo-re-na, che-ki.
(cheh-kee mawrey-nah cheh-kee

Che-ki mo-re-na, ¡Jue! ¿Que a
cheh-kee mawrey-nah huay kay

don-de esta ese rit-mo ca-ram-ba del me-re-cum-be?
dohn-day stah-sey reetmoh cah-ram-bah dehl meh-rey-koom-bey

Un pa-si-to a lan-te y o—tro pa-ra tras y
oon pah-see-toh ah lahn tey ee oh-troh pah-rah trahs ee

dan-do la vuel-ta dan-do la vuel-ta ¿Quién se que-da-ra? ¡Jue!
dahn-doh lah vwehl-tah dahn-doh lah vwehl-tah kee ehn sey kay-dah-rah huay)

Typical clave pattern:

How to play the game:

• One child is selected to dance in the middle of the circle. (A girl is *morena*, a boy is *moreno*.)

• The child steps sideways to the rhythm, left and then right, throughout.

• Girls place hands on hips, but boys may move more freely, usually without hands on the hips, but perhaps with one hand touching his midriff.

• The other children sing and clap on beats 1 and 3.
 In the second verse, the dancer moves forward and then backward.

• On the words *Y dando la vuelta*, the child closes and covers his/her eyes and rotates in place, pointing randomly. Whomever he or she points to as the song ends becomes the new dancer in the middle.

Further interpretation:

Alejandro Jimenez, a Puerto Rican musician who teaches music in Hartford, Connecticut, remembers an additional verse with a slightly different slant, from his childhood in Quebradillas, a small town on the northwest coast of the island. Substitute these lines for the first two lines of verse one:

El juez le dijo al cura
Y el cura le dijo al juez,
¿Que a donde...etc.

These lines translate as: The judge said to the priest, and the priest said to the judge, where's that...etc. The judge (representing civil law or custom), and the priest, (representing religious law or custom), are watching, gossiping about the dancer's hip motions—Uh oh! Are they too provocative, or do they stay within the bounds of propriety? In this largely Catholic country, it would be important to be enthusiastic in interpreting a rhythm with your body without going beyond what is considered proper in your community. This is especially true in a small town like Quebradillas. Ricardo's area of urban Santurce/San Juan might not be as conservative, and so this variant would not necessarily be heard there.

⤳Section 4
Europe

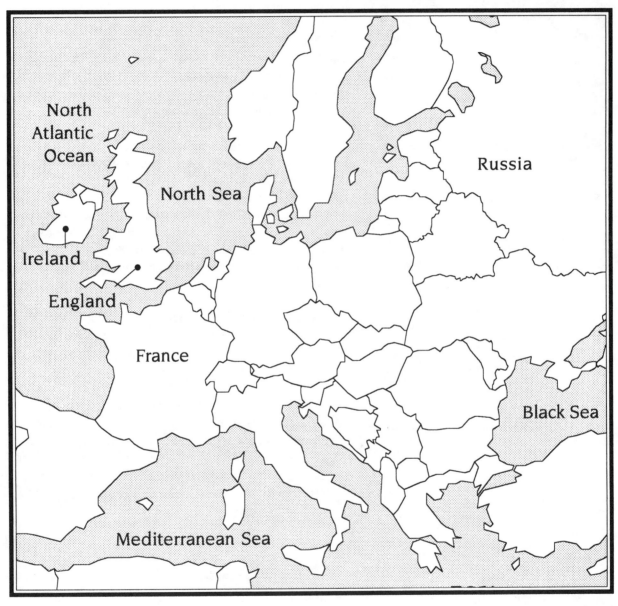

England
France
Ireland
Russia

England

Victoria and Dawn Chambers

"Most of the games we played
when I was young
had music to them.
They never seem to
go out of fashion.
My sister teaches
the same games to her young
pre-schoolers in South London.
We have an unbroken
twenty-six year old family
tradition!"

- Dawn Chambers

Dawn Chambers walked to school on streets paved with history and filled with the sounds of children singing. Born within hearing distance of St. Peter's, Whitechapel, St. Aldgate, and St. John's churches in London, she loved to hear the great bells mark the hour, as they have for centuries.

Children everywhere have their own culture—songs and rhymes, many of them centuries old—which they pass down to one another. Dawn, at ten years of age, became an enthusiastic music teacher to her baby sister Victoria, instructing her in the songs and games she herself loved so much.

Their house in the country was always alive with music. Not owning a television, they were avid fans of a radio program "Listen to Mother" that featured nursery rhymes, stories and songs.

Starting with the recorder at six, she moved on to piano lessons at age ten. She received a Bachelor of Music degree with honors from Birmingham University in England, then earned a Bachelor of Music Education and a Master of Music degree from the University of New Mexico as well.

Dawn married an American and settled in the United States, but she continues to observe many of her favorite childhood traditions. She strings paper garlands through her house during the Christmas season, and decorates the trees in her yard with tinsel. She drinks several cups of strong tea each day, and bakes English-style mincemeat pies, scones, custard and shortbread. Easter demands fresh and sticky hot cross buns. Her garden is reminiscent of her childhood home, with broad and runner beans fighting for space, and bright with the Madam Hardy roses that grew in her yard in England.

Thatched Cotswold cottages, vine covered medieval castles and centuries-old stone churches dot the English countryside. Neat rose gardens line village paths, and heather grows wild on the moors. These fairy tale images contrast with the stark brick mill and factory buildings of the Midlands manufacturing region, birthplace of the Industrial Revolution.

Described by Shakespeare as a "precious stone set in the sea" the English Channel and North Sea serve as a moat between England and the European mainland. Nonetheless, England was descended upon in 700 B.C. by a group of Celtic people from central and western Europe who called themselves Britons. Julius Caesar invaded in 55 B.C. and for over 400 years, England was part of the Roman Empire. In the larger towns people spoke Latin and lived as the Romans did. When the Roman Empire weakened, England was open to invasion by Norse and Germanic warriors including the Angles, Saxons, and Jutes. Following several shifts of power, the Normans, led by William of Normandy finally conquered England in 1066. Crowned King William I of England, he was first in a lengthy lineage of kings and queens that reaches to the present day.

Great Britain is officially referred to as the United Kingdom of Great Britain and Northern Ireland. The U.K. includes England (the largest part of Great Britain), Northern Ireland (Ulster), Scotland, Wales, the Channel Islands, and the Isle of Man. The English people are of mixed Celtic, Roman, Anglo-Saxon and Norman origin, although there are many other European, Asian and Afro-Caribbean people now living in Great Britain. The Anglican "Church of England" is the established church, although many other Christian denominations flourish, as well as a large Jewish community. The government is a constitutional monarchy, with Queen Elizabeth II currently at the head (functioning primarily in a ceremonial capacity), and a Prime Minister heading up a Parliament, consisting of the House of Lords and House of Commons, actually governing on a day-to-day basis.

Another famous Briton, Mother Goose, may or may not have actually existed herself, but characters from her rhymes are alive in the imaginations of English- speaking children everywhere. With a cast of characters that includes an unfortunate egg and a merry old king, some of these rhymes were being chanted as early as the seventeenth century. The rhymes, it's said, were originally intended for adult consumption, with childish verse disguising biting political satire. But that has been lost, and now they are within the domain of children's verse, one of England's more eccentric contributions to world literature.

Birthplace to Shakespeare as well as the Beatles, England's influence on literature and music has been felt the world over. A strong

oral tradition influenced even the classical composers, who were inspired in many cases by folk tunes and dances. Benjamin Britten and Ralph Vaughn Williams are two good examples. England has a rich tradition of music and dance linked to the changing seasons of the agrarian year. Morris dancers, wearing pads of bells strapped to their legs, waving white handkerchiefs and brandishing sticks "wake up the earth" on May Day. The dances have their origins in pre-Christian fertility rites. Crops are said to grow as high as the dancers are able to leap. Mummer's plays in which the character of Saint George, England's patron, is ritually slain by sword dancers and brought to life again are performed at Christmas, suggesting the rebirth of the winter solstice sun. English ritual dances are also performed in the United States which currently has close to 200 active Morris teams. Traditional instruments used to accompany these songs and dances include the pipe and tabor (a kind of drum), fiddles, bagpipes, concertina, and melodian (a type of accordion). Perhaps the best known collector and publisher of British folksongs, street cries, chanteys, children's songs, ballads, and traditional dances is Cecil Sharpe.

In the early seventeenth century colonists from the British Isles settled in America's Appalachian Mountain area, bringing with them a wealth of tunes, many of them hauntingly modal. The isolation of the area prevented outside influence and traditional tunes and words were preserved in their original form for many years. In some Appalachian hamlets, people were still using obsolete Elizabethan phrases well into the twentieth century. Cecil Sharpe spent years in the Appalachians, collecting songs that had been barely touched by time.

Oranges and Lemons

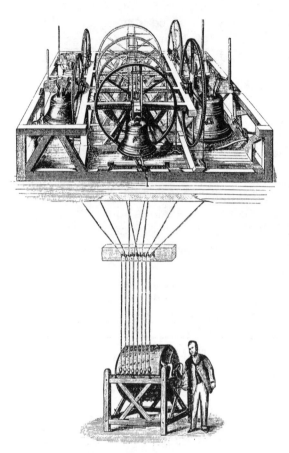

"**O**ranges and Lemons" is a favorite party game of young English children. The bells referred to in the song are from the many churches in the city of London. Bells are considered to have individual personalities and, traditionally, a bell is given a name prior to being rung for the first time. Each church bell in England has it's own particular phrase to "speak." In addition, the people of a parish associate themselves with the sound of the parish bell. A person described as having been born "within the sound of Bow bells" is identified as a Cockney.

The lyrics refer to prisoners being held in the Tower of London, which was built in the twelfth century. Prior to execution they were marched through the city as a gruesome reminder of what was in store for lawbreakers and debtors. Church bells rang to mark the progress of their final march through the streets. The candle in the last verse belongs to the priest who administered last rites to the prisoners. The chopper is, of course, their executioner.

Dawn remembers singing the first verse over and over until each child collapsed after the tug of war! The second verse is not widely known.

Lyrics:
"Oranges and lemons," say the bells of St. Clements!
"I owe you five farthings," say the bells of St. Martin's.
"When will you pay me?" say the bells of Old Bailey.
"When I grow rich," say the bells of Shoreditch.
"When will that be?" say the bells of Stepney,
"I do not know," says the great bell of Bow.
Here comes a candle to light you to bed,
And here comes a chopper to chop off your head!

"Pancakes and fritters," say the bells of St. Peter's.
"Two sticks and an apple," say the bells of Whitechapel.
"Old Father Baldpate," say the bells of St. Aldgate.
"Poker and tongs," say the bells of St. John's.
"Kettles and pans," say the bells of St. Ann's
"Brickbats and tiles," say the bells of St. Giles!
Here comes a candle to light you to bed,
And here comes a chopper to chop off your head!

∿ Extensions

1. The song may be enjoyed independently of the game. Divide the children in two, with lots of space between the groups if possible. The groups then sing alternate lines, to give the effect of the bells answering one another over a distance.

2. The melody moves up and down a lot, like the sound of bells ringing. Listen, then sing, while patting the beat.

Oranges and Lemons

19

"Oranges and le-mons," say the bells of St. Clements! "I owe you five far-things," say the bells of St. Mar-tins. "When will you pay me?" say the bells of Old Bai-ley. "When I grow rich," say the bells of Shore-ditch. "When will that be?" say the bells of Step-ney. "I do not know," says the great bell of Bow. Here comes a can-dle to light you to bed, and here comes a chop-per to chop off your head!

Singing Game Directions:

• After deciding in secret which one will be the orange and which one the lemon, two children stand and form an arch with their arms, "London Bridge" style.

• The other children form a line and skip under.

• On "chopper," the two children forming an arch chant "chop, chop, chop, chop" continuously until they select a child to try to catch (by lowering their joined hands over the child's head.) The idea is to surprise the "victim." Once "chopped," the victim decides if s/he will be an orange or a lemon, then whispers this decision to the choppers, who reveal their identities to him/her. If lemon, for example, s/he will stand behind and wrap his/her arms around the waist of the chopper who is lemon. Likewise for orange.

• When every child has been "chopped," and is lined up on the two sides, a tug-of-war ensues between the oranges and lemons.

Oh My Little Sixpence

"Oh, My Little Sixpence" is an English song found in early Mother Goose collections. Intrigued as a child by the words, Dawn learned this tune from her mother.

The song is a good introduction to the old British monetary system of pounds, shillings and pence. There were 20 shillings to a pound and 12 pence to a shilling. A sixpence is worth six British pennies or a half a shilling. English brides put a sixpence in their shoe for luck. Dawn says that the English Tooth Fairy always left a shilling under her pillow! The fourpence (groat) and twopence (tuppence) were other denominations.

There were also threepenny coins and even a penny was divisible into halfpennies (pronounced "haypennys") and farthings. When Dawn was in high school, the monetary system was converted to the decimal system, with 100 pennies to the pound.

Lyrics:
O my little sixpence, I love sixpence,
I love sixpence better that my life.
I spent a penny of it, I lent another of it,
I carried fourpence home to my wife.

O my little fourpence, I love fourpence,
I love fourpence better than my life
I spent a penny of it, I lent another of it,
I carried tuppence home to my wife.

O my little tuppence, I love tuppence,
I love tuppence better than my life,
I spent a penny of it, I lent another of it,
I carried nothing home to my wife.

O my little nothing, I love nothing,
I love nothing better than my life!
I cannot spend it, I cannot lend it;
Oh I love nothing better than my wife.

Extensions

1. The melancholy feeling is created by the minor mode. A guitar provides the accompaniment.

2. Encourage the children to bring in foreign coins and paper money. Compare size, weight, color and value, as well as value in US dollars. (Many newspapers publish the conversion from foreign currency to US dollars on the business pages.)

3. Do the "money math" in the song on the blackboard.

Oh My Little Sixpence

Oh my lit-tle six-pence, I love six - pence, I love six-pence

bet-ter than my life.   I spent a penny of it, I lent a-no-ther of it,

I   car-ried four - pence   home   to   my wife.

France

Richard Hiester as a young child

"I was raised by a French mother
and American father,
and feel that I am truly bicultural,
not only in my language
but also in my way of thinking.
I had a wonderful
French childhood
in the United States!
From the food, to the wine,
to the intellectual discussions
around the dinner table,
and of course the music.
We sang constantly.
I am raising my children
in the same way."

- Richard Hiester

Richard Hiester's grandmother, Suzanne Dessertenne, taught him many French songs when he was a little boy as well as the history of her family name. At one time Dessertenne was spelled DeSertenne, an aristocratic name. It was changed shortly after the French Revolution in order to keep the family safe from the guillotine!

Richard's father was an American working for the French Underground in World War II when he met the Parisian woman he fell in love with and married. Although Richard was born and raised in the United States, he spent most family vacations—and his honeymoon!—staying with aunts, uncles and cousins in France. His parents maintained a bilingual, bicultural, household, with French spoken at home and English everywhere else. His mother used French recipes for all her cooking, and dinners included a bit of fine wine even for the children, lots of dishes with sauces and subtle flavors, and lengthy conversations around the table. They celebrated both the Fourth of July and French Independence Day—July 14. For the feast of Premier de L'An (First of the Year) the family exchanged presents, and at Christmas his *sabot*, or shoe, waited by the fireplace to be filled with small presents. He is raising his own children to be bicultural in the same way.

When Richard was a child, he and his family sang at every opportunity. The family car was their rehearsal hall on wheels, as they often sang en route to their destinations. Richard's father would teach all of them a melody and then each child would learn a different accompaniment part in turn. His parents and his three siblings sang so much that they jokingly referred to themselves as the French "Von Trapp Family Singers." They performed as a family for a variety of social events, and many of their selections were French songs. His father was a tenor, choir director and Director of the Denver Opera Theater for nine years, and their home was a stopover for many French performers on tour.

Richard is currently the Program Director of Adolescent Programs at Memorial Psychiatric Hospital in Albuquerque, New Mexico. He also maintains a private practice in psychotherapy.

Richard's French grandmother, Suzanne Dessertenne.

France, the largest nation in western Europe, is hexagonally shaped and almost completely surrounded by natural boundaries. These include the North Sea and English Channel, Atlantic Ocean, Pyrenees Mountains, Mediterranean Sea, Alps, Jura Mountains and Rhine River. The landscape is rich and varied, from the grape orchards of the wine country to the snowy Pyrenees. The national language is French, and Roman Catholicism is the main religion.

A republic, France is the fifth largest economic power in the world and a major producer of agricultural and dairy products (in particular, wheat and cheeses), wine, steel and technology. France claims the fastest train in the world, the TGV (for *trés gran vitesse,* meaning "very great speed"), and is the world's fourth largest automobile producer turning out Renaults, Citroens and Peugeots for the international market. The minority population in France includes Africans, Iberians, Southern Europeans, Eastern Europeans, Arabs and Asians.

In Paris tourists climb the Eiffel tower and visit Notre Dame Cathedral, a masterpiece of Gothic Art. Home of the Louvre, one of the world's greatest museums, the French artistic influence has been felt around the world. What aspiring painter hasn't dreamed of sitting in a Parisian cafe, discussing Toulouse Lautrec over a carafe of wine? Or sketching in Monet's garden? Degas, Cezanne, Renoir - the great French painters are too numerous to mention, but all were inspired by France's sun bathed landscape and the night life of her cities.

French composers have had a major influence on Western classical music. The great French composers all took inspiration from the lovely and varied folk music of the French people. Debussy, Ravel and Faure have made a rich musical contribution with their impressionistic works. Parisian cafes and clubs are home to jazz musicians from around the world, poets, writers and heated late night discussions about life and politics. (African-American jazz musicians commonly found acceptance of their music in France long before jazz was considered an important musical genre in the United States.)

Napoleon Bonaparte, Joan of Arc, and Charlemagne each had an impact on the history of the world. French philosophers and writers including Jean-Jacques Rousseau, Victor Hugo and Jean Paul Sartre colored its thinking. French clothing style and cuisine are copied worldwide. The *avant garde* elsewhere is the norm in France, and the spirit of the country is simply irrepressible.

French aristocrats of the Napoleonic era

﹏All about
Ainsi Font, Font, Font

The Little Marionettes

"**A**insi font font font" is a popular French song and finger play. It describes a marionette that turns and turns and turns and then goes away, only to come back again when the children fall asleep. A marionette is a puppet that is controlled by a series of strings. One is attached to the head, one to the shoulders, etc. It makes jerky movements when brought to life by the puppeteer.

Lyrics:
Ainsi font font font
Les petites marionettes
Ainsi font font font
Trois petits tours puis elles s'en vont.

Mais elles reviendront
Les petites marionettes
Mais elles reviendront
Quand les enfants dormiront.

Translation:
This is how they turn, turn, turn
   (*lit.* Here's how they do it.)
The little marionettes
This is how they turn turn turn
Three little turns then off they go.

But they come right back
The little marionettes
Bu they come right back
When the children go to sleep.

﹏ Extensions

1. *Marionette* is the French word for the wooden segmented puppets hung from strings, also called marionettes in English. Many words came directly from the French like this, or are Anglicized. Think of others with the children: croissant—crescent-shaped flaky rolls; barrette—hair clip; ballet—ballet; crepes—thin pancakes.

2. While listening to the song, make the motions of the marionettes turning on their strings, running away after three turns, and coming back. Pairs of children can dramatize the roles of the puppeteer and the marionette.

3. Sing the song and pat the beat with your hands, noting the ritard (slowing down) at the end of the song.

5. Play the game (see directions below music transcription).

Ainsi Font, Font, Font
(The Little Marionettes)

Ain - si font font font les pe - ti - tes ma - rio - net - tes, Ain - si
(an - see fohn fohn fohn lay p' teet-uh mar - yoh net - uh an - see

font font font trois petits tours puis elles s'en vont. Mais elles re - viendront les pe-
fohn fohn fohn twah p'tee toor pwees - el - sahn-vohn mayz- ehl ruh veean drohn lay p'

ti - tes mari - o - net - tes, mais elles re - vien dront quand les en fants dor- mi ront.
teet - uh mar - yoh net - uh mayz - ehl ruh - veean drohn kahn lays ahn-fahn dohr- meer ohn)

Motions for the finger play:

1. Relatives or those working with very young children may seat the child on the adult's lap. Otherwise, the adult may simply stand or sit facing the child.

2. During the first three measures, the adult waves their own hands back and forth in opposite directions, like a jerky marionette, with hands held in a claw-like shape.

3. During the fourth measure, the hands are turned three times then quickly hidden behind the adult's back.

4. During the next three measures, the hands slowly reappear from behind the adult's back, using the same claw-like shape.

5. On the last measure the hands swoop down to give a gentle tickle or hug to the child; or, if more appropriate, to wiggle the fingers wildly in front of the child's face.

Ireland

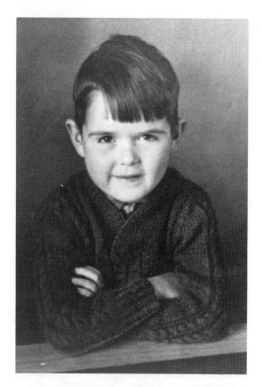

Gerard Leonard as a child

"One of my fondest memories is going to visit my grandmother. Every time I went to her house, she wouldn't let me go home without giving her a few waltzes around the kitchen! My childhood was rich with singing and dancing. What a gift it was...and is!"

- Gerard Leonard

When Gerard Leonard completed his Montessori training in Dublin in 1981, he intended to work abroad for a year or two, possibly in India or Japan. Qualified to teach internationally, Gerard applied to a number of schools world-wide. Following an overseas telephone interview with a school in Litchfield, Connecticut, he was hired three days before the semester began. Originally here on a three-year cultural exchange, Gerard grew to love the United States and decided to continue his career here.

Both he and his wife Kathleen Allen teach at "The Montessori School" in Wilton, Connecticut. Gerard works with the lower elementary age children, and his wife with the upper elementary group. Since their daughter Hannah is a member of the nursery class, the entire family sets out for school together each day.

A native of Dublin Ireland where people "really do sing in the pubs," Gerard brings "street songs" (traditional folk songs) as well as lullabies to his classroom. His parents are from County West meath, from the village of Delvin, where music is heard as much out on the roads as in the homes and pubs.

Many of the songs and dances he uses were learned from his mother and grandmother. When he was a child his grandmother liked to put *céilí* music on the radio and dance with him around the kitchen. Although *céilí* is the name given to Irish dance music, his grandmother used the term in another way as well. He remembers her inviting neighbors to "come in and have a *céilí*" meaning "come in and have a chat." His grandmother and his great aunt Molly grew up in what was known as a "*céilí* house," one in which neighbors came to sing and dance informally, sometimes every evening! An old farmhouse, the open hearth was so large you could actually walk in to it and sit on little low hearth stools called *furums*. It was hard to sit still however, when the music of fiddles, tin whistles, mandolins, melodeons and voices filled the air.

"Give us a song" is the phrase Irish people use to request a ballad. The lengthy Irish ballads Gerard sometimes shares with his students are as much story as song. The children enjoy singing with him, both in Gaelic and English. Although he can speak the language, Gaelic is not Gerard's mother tongue.

With the exception of Aran Islanders and those born in Connaught, Donegal and Kerry on the west coast, few Irish today speak Gaelic as their mother tongue. After several centuries of fierce resistance to English incursion, Ireland was finally subdued in the 1600s. Attempting to break the spirit of a people who revered their poets as much as their kings, laws were enacted which made it a crime to speak Gaelic. Farmers were turned off their land and forced west to the rocky soil of Connaught and County Clare when the rich pasture-land east of the Shannon River was commandeered for British settlers. The British strong-hold fanned out from the city of Dublin, an area known as "the pale." The Gaelic language was kept alive by native speakers living "beyond the pale" on the west coast where the Irish chieftains still held sway. To this day, many people of Celtic ancestry take pride in being able to speak or sing even a little bit of Gaelic, knowing how close their language came to annihilation.

Referred to as "Irish," the Gaelic language has been a required subject in school since the nation regained its independence and became the Irish Free State in 1921. The country was partitioned at this time, with Northern Ireland remaining under British rule, a decision that has been bitterly disputed since.

During the nineteenth century a large influx of people from Ireland arrived in the United States. Native Irish at this time were prohibited from owning land in their own country, or receiving an education. Farmers were so heavily taxed that, although they raised several crops, virtually everything, save the potato crop, went in rent and taxes. When a blight hit the potato crop, severe famine ensued. Although confronted at first with prejudice in the United States, years of hard work saw the Irish move into positions of leadership in the American workplace.

Known as Eire in Gaelic, the island is located in the North Atlantic Ocean. Warmed by the Gulf Stream, Ireland has a mild, moist climate. In some areas of the island, people need their umbrellas as many as 200 days a year. When the sun is out long enough to burn off the legendary Irish mist, the views are beautiful. Ancient stone walls surround miles of green fields where dairy cattle graze. Fields of oats, wheat, barley, turnips, sugarbeets, and potatoes are evidence of an economy still based on agriculture. Viewed by some as almost a symbol of the nation, the potato is actually an American native, imported to Ireland by Sir Walter Raleigh for experimental cultivation.

The true symbol of Ireland, shown bright and shiny on every Irish penny, is the harp or *clairseach*. In ancient Irish society, the harper was second in importance only to the king. More than a musician, the harper, or bard, was a guardian of the nation's history and mythic traditions which were preserved in verse. The harper's skill at weaving a spell with music and recitation was seen as a divine gift.

The harp, along with the concertina, fiddle, tin whistle and *uilleann* (elbow) pipes are the primary instruments of traditional Irish music, backed up by the rousing beat of the *bodhran* frame drum as it is struck by the distinctively carved stick called a *tipper*. Irish "step dancing" is performed with intricate, lively foot-work in cleated shoes, with a stiff upper body posture. Lively jigs and reels contrast with poignant love ballads, biting political and topical folk songs, rock music that strongly shows its roots, and ballads weaving tales of enchantment. Well-known performers include the Clancy Brothers, the Chieftains, the Bothy Band, Dolores Keane, Clannad, the Black Family, Planxty, Patrick Ball, Robin Williamson, Noirin Ni Riain, Sinead O'Connor and U2.

Ireland's people today number approximately 3,500,000, but so many have emigrated in the past, that there are actually more Irish-descended people living outside of the country than in. Not long ago, children growing up in New York City were told to watch for the leprechauns and fairies said to have come over on the same boats that brought their grandparents to this country. Cast like a handful of grain out over the world, their legends and musical heritage have nourished the Irish people wherever they have taken root.

~All about
Éiníní

Little Birds

An Irish lullaby Gerard learned as a child, "Éiníní" gently invites a group of little birds to go to sleep. In Irish the syllable "ín" (pronounced "een") means little. When added to the end of a word, "ín" changes its meaning. For example the word *bothar* means road. A *bothairín* (pronounced "boreen") would be a little road. Gerard sings this song with both the children in his class and with his own daughter, Hannah.

Gaelic Pronunciation

- Roll "r" slightly.

- "d" is almost a th sound. *The tongue is thrust forward against the top front teeth.*

- "ch" is slightly gutteral. *The sound does not come from down in the throat, but rather at the back of the palate.*

Lyrics: *See transcription for phonetic pronunciation.*
Éiníní éiníní, codailígí codailígí (2x)
Codailígí, codailígí, cois a 'claí'muigh cois a
   'claí'muigh,
Codailígí, codailígí, cois a 'claí'muigh cois a
   'claí'muigh.

Éiníní éiníní, codailígí codailígí (2x)
An londubh 's an fiach dubh, téigí a chodladh, téigí a
   chodladh,
An chéirseach 's an préachán, téigí a chodladh, téigí a
   chodladh.

Translation:
Little birds, little birds, go to sleep, go to sleep (2x)
Go to sleep, go to sleep by the fence outside,
by the fence outside (2x)

Little birds, little birds, go to sleep, go to sleep (2x)
The blackbird and the crow fall asleep, fall asleep
The song thrush and the raven fall asleep, fall asleep.

~ Extensions

1. Attach *ín* to the end of children's names, as is characteristic in Ireland. For example, Moire or Maura (Gaelic for Mary) + *ín* (een) becomes Moirin or Maureen.

2. While listening, pat the pulse, accenting the first of every three beats.

3. Rock gently from side to side while singing softly but expressively, as if to lull a baby to sleep.

4. Create motions to use while singing, such as gently flapping bird wings with the hands, and hands under a tilted head for "go to sleep."

Éiníní
(*Little Birds*)

Éi - ní - ní éi - ní - ní, co-dai - lí - gí co-dai - lí - gí. Éi -
(Ay - nee-nee ay - nee-nee, cuh-duh - lee - ghee, cuh-duh - lee - ghee Ay -

ní - ní éi - ní - ní, co-dai - lí - gí co-dai - lí - gí. **1.** Co-dai-
nee - nee ay - nee-nee, cuh-duh-lee - ghee, cuh-duh-lee - ghee cuh-duh-

2. An
(uhn

lí - gí co-dai-lí - gí, cois a `claí-`muigh cois a `claí-`muigh. Co-dai-
lee - ghee, cuh-duh-lee - ghee kuhsh uh kly - mwih kuhsh uh kly - mwih cuh-duh-

lon-dubh 's an fi-ach dubh Téi-gí a chod ladh, Téi-gí a chodladh, An
lun - duhv ihs uhn fee-uch duhv tchaygee (c)huh - luh tchay-gee (c)huh - luh uhn

lí - gí codai-lí - gí, cois a `claí-`muigh cois a `claí-`muigh.
lee - ghee, cuhduh-lee - ghee kuhsh uh kly - mwih kuhsh uh kly - mwih)

chéir-seach 'san pré-a chán Téi - gí a chod - ladh, Téi-gí a chod - ladh.
cheeayr-shuch ihs uhn pray-uh-chahn tchay-gee (c)huh - luh tchay-gee (c)huh - luh)

All about
An Madairín Rua

The Little Red Fox

"An Madairín Rua" was taught to Gerard by his mother, Pauline, when he was quite young. It tells the story of the sly little fox who not only steals the farmer's goose but brazenly feasts on it, and even invites the farmer to join him! The song is traditionally sung in a mix of Irish and English lyrics.

Lyrics:: *See transcription for phonetic pronunciation*
Chorus: An madairín arua, rua, rua, rua, rua
An madairín arua tá gránna
An madairín arua 'na luisa lua chair,
'S barr a dhá chluais in, áirde

Verse 1: Ar ghabháil ó thuaidh dom trí Shliabh Luachra
'Gus mise cur tuairisc mo ghéanna,
Ar mo chasadh aduaidh, sea fuair mé a dtuairisc
Go raibh Madairín Rua á n-aoireacht.

Verse 2: Good Morrow, fox, good morrow, Sir
Pray what is that you're eating?
A fine fat goose that I stole from you,
and won't you come and taste it?

Verse 3: Oh, no indeed, ní mhaith liom í
Ní bhlaisfead pioc di ar aon chor
But I vow and I swear you'll dearly pay
For my fine fat goose you're eating!

Translation:
Chorus: The little red, red, red, red, red fox,
the little red fox is naughty.
The little red fox, is lying in the rushes
And the tips of his ears peek out above.

Verse 1: As I went to the north through Mount Luachra
And I, looking for my geese,
As I turned from the north (toward the south) I found out the news,
That the little red fox was herding them!

Verse 2 is in English

Verse 3: Oh, no indeed, I don't wish any (of her)
I would not taste a bit of her at all, at all
(the rest is in English)

Extensions

1. Learn the Gaelic chorus. Listen to Gerry sing verse one, and then join in on the remaining choruses and verses.

2. Learn and use these Irish words in conversation:
madairín - fox
rua - red
luachair - rushes

An Madairín Rua

(The Little Red Fox)

(Chorus) An ma-dair-ín a-rua, rua, rua, rua, rua, An
[Ahn muh - (d)ah-reen ah - roo roo roo roo roo ahn

1. Ar gha-bhá-il ó thuaidh dom trí Shliabh Luachra 'Gus
Er guw - ah - wil oh whoih duhm tree shleeuhv loo(ch)r gus

ma-dair-ín a-rua tá grán - na. An Ma-dair-ín a-rua 'na
muh - (d)ah reen ah - roo tah grahn - nah ahn muh-(d)ah-reen ah - roo nah

mis - e cur tuairisc mo ghean - na Ar mo - cha-sadh aduaidh, sea
mish - uh cur toorishk(uh) muh gay - nah er moo (ch)uhsah adoo shah

lui - sa lua-chair, 'S barr a dhá chluais in,
lee - sah loor - hiss bahr - ah dah - (ch)loo - sihn

fuair mé a dtuairisc Go raibh Ma-dair in - arua a
foor may a doorishk guh rev mah - (d)ah - reen a - roo aw

áir - de **2.** Good mor - row fox, Good mor - row, Sir. Pray
ahr je]
3. Oh, no in - deed, ní mhaith lion í, ní
n'aoir - eacht. [nee wah luhm ee nee
nay(o)r - o(ch)t

what is that you're eat - ing? A fine fat goose that I
bhlais-fead pioc di ar aon chor But I vow and I swear you'll
vlos - fid pyuck dih er ayun (ch)uhr]

stole from you, and won't you come and taste it?
dear - ly pay For my fine fat goose you're eat - ing!

Add a drumming pattern for a frame drum: 𝄆 ♪. ♪ ♪. ♪ ♩ ♩ ♩ ♩ 𝄇

85

Russia

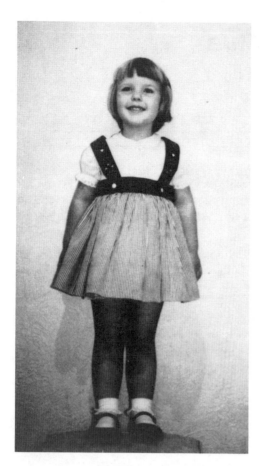

Beth Cohen as a child

*"I fondly remember
my mother singing to me
when I was growing up.
She sang a wide variety of songs
and many
were Russian folk melodies.
My favorite was
'Ochi Chornia' (Black Eyes).
My mother would sing it
all around the house,
when cooking dinner
and when we were
'hanging out' together."*

- Beth Cohen

(*Beth Cohen and Katya Ponomareva are two women whose links to Russian music have taken them on a journey to understand their heritage more fully. Beth, a second-generation Russian-Jewish American, has returned to her cultural roots by studying the music she remembered hearing and loving as a child. Katya, a young Russian from Saransk, has shared her knowledge of her homeland by offering others the music she has been immersed in for her lifetime.*)

Beth Cohen never met her grandparents, and yet they had a profound effect on her direction in life. Her maternal grandparents were Russian Jews. Her paternal grandfather was a Lithuanian Jew, and her paternal grandmother was a Polish Jew. Her parents came to this country without them, bringing photos with Russian writing on them, a beloved samovar and other odds and ends of the "old country," and, most importantly, bringing memories of Bubbeh and Zeydie to tell. Raised in a traditional Jewish home in Newton, Massachusetts, where English and Yiddish were spoken, but not Polish or Russian, Beth learned a few Yiddish songs from her mother, as well as the Russian songs her grandfather had entertained her mother with, including the popular song included here, "Kalinka."

As Beth delved into the family history she began to desire a deeper understanding of and connection to the culture of her European grandparents who remained behind while their children journeyed to a new life in America. Eight years ago, she found that connection when she began singing with Svirka, an Eastern European women's chorus. Performing a wide repertoire of Eastern European material, Beth often accompanies the group on her mandolin balalaika, a Romanian string instrument similar to the triangular Russian balalaika but with a double course of strings.

Beth has a B.M. degree in voice performance and gives private voice, balalaika, guitar and mandolin lessons. Her performance style is rich and emotional, and she particularly enjoys singing in Russian, with as much *schmaltz* (emotion) as possible in her renditions. Beth believes we need to make a positive connection to our cultural roots in order to reach our full creative potential, and feels that her work with Svirka has given her tremendous insight into her own heritage.

Ekaterina "Katya" Ponomareva

*"I love going to summer camp,
even now.
In the evening someone will start
walking through the woods,
playing accordion as he walks.
Gradually people come out
of the buildings and walk
and jump and run with him,
singing the whole way to the pond
where we sit
around a huge bonfire
and sing until very late."*

- Katya Ponomareva

Ekaterina "Katya" Ponomareva was born in 1976 in Saransk, a city in the small republic inside of Russia called Mordovia. Her mother Tanya was from Siberia, and her father, Alexander, from the Volga region. Both parents are computer programmers. She grew up and lives in a high-ceilinged flat of three rooms on the fourth floor of an old building. It has a kitchen, two bedroom/living rooms and a bathroom. Her middle-class family is lucky because they also have a large walk-in closet that is used for storage, as a quiet place to be alone, or as an extra bedroom in case overnight guests arrive.

Saransk is a beautiful old area, with forests in and around it. Foxes still live in the forests, and have become the symbol of the city. During the summer the temperature averages approximately 70 degrees, and during the winter the days typically hit twenty-below zero, sometimes colder. Winters always bring a good deal of snow, and so Katya's father took her cross country skiing in the forests from an early age.

For several summers Katya went to a special camp in Saransk where she learned games, how to put on musical shows, and how to organize and direct the efforts of a group of people. In the evening the campers would sit together and sing, and sometimes travelling folksingers would come to the camp and share songs and stories.

She has travelled quite a bit, both within Russia and to other parts of the world. Her grandmother lives near Volga, and a few times they have spent several days on a ship, sailing from city to city on the Volga River.

One of her favorite experiences was taking part in the "Role Games" in the forests near Moscow. These are games that large numbers of people of all ages join. Participants dress in costumes they have created, sometimes working for a whole year on them. They "become" literary or fantasy characters, including many from Tolkien's work, and live the parts for a week or so.

Katya is now a student at the local University in Saransk, studying languages. She began learning English in second grade, and also speaks French. She helped to create and performed in a show with a group of Russian and American teenagers sponsored by an international performing arts exchange program, Creative Response of Virginia (formerly known as Peace Child), then had an opportunity to stay with a family in Delaware for three weeks. They invited her to return for the 1993-94 school year. While in the States, she continued to take part in musical theatre productions. She enjoys languages, playing guitar, and singing folksongs with friends.

Matryoshka are round and colorful wooden nesting dolls, well-known throughout Russia and familiar now to children in many countries. The typical Matryoshka consists of seven wooden dolls beautifully hand-painted in traditional clothing and designs, graduated in size so they fit together perfectly. The largest doll opens up to reveal a smaller doll, which also opens up, all the way down to the tiniest doll at the very core. Today, Matryoshka are sold that depict political figures as well as women with modest scarves tied around their hair and wearing flower-strewn aprons.

Like the Russian Matryoshka, the Commonwealth of Independent States is made up of many different layers. Formerly referred to as Russia, the U.S.S.R or the Soviet Union, the Commonwealth spans one-sixth of the surface of the earth and includes significant parts of two continents, making it the largest country in the world. The territory stretches from the European port city of St. Petersburg to the Pacific port of Vladivostock, crossing eleven time zones. When the sun is setting in Moscow, it is rising over the Pacific coast towns. Although we often think of Russia as cold, parts of the country in central Asia experience some of the highest temperatures on earth: up to 140 degrees Fahrenheit. And, on the other extreme, with much of its country lying within the Arctic circle, Russia is no stranger to freezing winters: temperatures of -70 degrees Fahrenheit are regularly recorded!

Russia is traversed by the Ural Mountains which separate Asia from Europe. There are rich deposits of valuable minerals in these mountains, including uranium which is used in atomic energy plants, and coal, which is burned for energy. Experts think that Russia also has more petroleum deposits than any other nation.

Russia's vast stretch of land can be thought of as really three horizontal belts of climate types. In the south, there are vast plains, called the *steppe*. In the middle, there are thick forests with tremendous supplies of timber. And in the north, the frozen tundra where the ground is covered by permafrost and remains frozen summer as well as winter. Indigenous tribes, similar to what Americans call Eskimos, travel across the frozen land in sleds and raise herds of Reindeer. Russia is the closest country to the United States, after Mexico and Canada— Alaska is a few miles across the Bering Strait.

Over 150 different nationalities including Russians, Ukrainians, Mongolians, Georgians, Uzbekians, Armenians, Estonians, Latvians and Lithuanians are represented in its population and member-states, with each state named for its predominant ethnic group—Russia, Latvia, etc. Although Russian was at one time the official language, well over one hundred languages and dialects are actually spoken.

As long ago as 1682, when Peter the Great (who as an adult was almost seven feet tall) was named tsar, laws outlawing many of the old traditions of Russia were passed, at an attempt to modernize Russia. Many priests would not change their religious traditions and were forced to flee east to Siberia, and even Alaska where colonies of "Old Believers" still live today. Under the *tsars* (from the word "Caesar"), certain religious observations were discouraged, yet frequently practiced in secret at some peril. As Russia grew and changed, an aristocracy bloomed that revolved around the arts. Prompted perhaps by the intensity of historical events, the times inspired Russian writers including Pushkin, Tolstoy, Dostoevsky and Chekhov, artists Chagall and Kandinsky, and the composers Tchaikovsky, Rimskii-Korsakov, Mussorgsky and Prokofiev, still enjoyed worldwide.

Life for peasants and serfs was far less comfortable. They often lived in one-room huts which were cold in winter and stifling in summer. The warmest place to sleep was on the wood stove, and this was usually reserved for a visitor, the oldest member of the family, or a sick child. The life of the Russian peasant was filled with rituals and festivities that mirrored the seasons of the year, including Christmas celebrated on January 6 with stories of Father Frost (Dyed Moroz) and his helper the Snow Maiden (Snegoruchka) who would bring presents from the three magi to good children. In late summer the harvest was celebrated by tossing a bundle of hay dressed as a person into a river. Children were warned to be good or Baba Yaga, old "Bony Legs" would come and take them away to her house which sits on large chicken feet. Visitors were welcomed with customary Russian hospitality: bread (that which makes life possible) and salt (that which makes it bearable).

By the end of the 19th century, the lowly position of the serfs became a sore point between leaders and intellectuals who wanted freedom for everyone. A series of tsars came to power and were deposed until 1917, when Vladimir Ilych Lenin seized control and declared an atheist, communist state, promising "Bread, Peace and Land." A civil war erupted between the Communist Red Army and the troops of those loyal to the tsar. When Lenin died, Josef Stalin took charge, first preserving Lenin's body in a monumental tomb built in Red Square in 1923. People still wait in line to march silently past the encased body of the first Communist leader of Russia. Stalin classified people according to their nationality and created political subdivisions called "republics" which together made up a Union: the USSR. Russia was the largest state. Stalin held absolute power and jealously guarded that position by ordering mass killings and exiles. The "Stalinist terror" left somewhere between 30 and 50 million Russians dead or displaced, and yet the horror faced by Russians during the 1930s to 1950s was further exacerbated by World War II. Russia lost more people during this war than any other country—at least 20 million! Between Stalin and Hitler, almost an entire generation of Russians were wiped out.

Life in Communist Russia was ordered and predictable. Children entered school at age six, and wore uniforms to school. Most belonged to the Young Octobrist club and later the Young Pioneers, which are much like the Boy Scouts and Girl Scouts in America. Members wore red scarves and sometimes matching hats, went to camp to swim, fish, sing songs, and help farmers bring in the harvest. While most families, especially in the bigger cities, lived in small apartments and even sometimes shared the apartment with other families, many were able to acquire small shacks or houses outside of town called *dachas*. The government allowed people to keep only the things they grew on the land around their dachas, and therefore the entire yard of every one seemed like a thick garden of raspberries, strawberries, tomatoes, cucumbers, potatoes and other foods. These were the first signs of private property in the USSR, and are still in widespread use.

In 1985, Mikhail Gorbachev launched a three-pronged reform program: openness (*glasnost*), reconstruction (*perestroika*) and democratization. Openness led to freedom of speech, and by 1990, the Baltic republics declared they were no longer part of the USSR.

Soon other nationalities started demanding independence as well. When tsars ruled, the Orthodox Church was connected with the state and members of other religions, like Jews or Catholics, were often unwelcome in parts of Russia. As a result of Glasnost, many Jews emigrated to Israel, England and the United States.

Gorbachev's plan did not fare well. In 1990 and 1991 there were tremendous shortages in Moscow. Shopping for food might take two hours each day because many stores were empty, or stocked erratically. Gorbachev allowed open elections, and Yeltsin, a former Communist Party member, won. Rocky times continued with the attempted coup against Gorbachev in 1991, and the election of fifteen presidents for the fifteen republics of the USSR. Like political musical chairs, when the music stopped, Gorbachev was out, and Yeltsin remained. In late 1994, controversy over Russia's military invasion to squash the independence movement of the tiny republic of Chechnya proved unsettling to Yeltsin's popularity.

Fueled, perhaps, by the experience of being both allies toward the end of World War II, and "enemies" during the Cold War, the Russian and American people have long had a curiosity about each other's lifestyle, and an affection when personal encounters were made possible. Exchange programs between scientists, musicians and students abound. Russians are among the most highly educated people in the world, and the culture is a rich tapestry, filled with stories, folk dances and customs.

A popular folk instrument is the *balalaika*, a stringed instrument developed from its predecessor, the Tatar *dömra* at the beginning of the nineteenth century. The word *balalaika* is derived from a Russian term that means "chattering." Triangular in shape, the balalaika has three strings and comes in a variety of sizes from the soprano to the bass. Siberian legend has it that hunters, in search of sable and other fur bearing animals, play the balalaika for the forest spirits who reward them with good luck in their hunting.

Traditionally Russians wish one another good luck as if they were going on a hunt, saying: No fur, no feathers (*ni pukha ni pera*)—meaning go and get the whole beast (tackle the whole problem). To which the Russian reply is, spit on the ground and say "k chortu" (the devil can't stop me).

All about
Kalinka

Snowball Flowers

Russian Pronunciation

- zh - measure
- a - far
- e - yet
- i - keep
- o - short
- u - flute
- oo - cook
- *Accent marks show emphasis.*

"**K**alinka" is traditionally sung with lots of schmaltzy, exaggerated feeling. A classic Russian folk song, it is very gypsy-like in feeling. The word *kalinka* refers to a snowball bush, a green bush with puffy white flowers and bitter berries. *Malinka* is a raspberry bush with sweet berries used to make wine. The bitter and the sweet are both aspects of love.

Lyrics: (Transliteration)
Pod sosnoiu, pod zelenoiu,
Spat' polozhite vy menia.
Ai-liuli, liuli, Ai-liuli, liuli,
Spat' polozhite vy menia!

Kalinka, kalinka, kalinka moia!
V sadu iagoda malinka, malinka moia!
Kalinka, kalinka, kalinka moia!
V sadu iagoda malinka, malinka moia! Akh!

Krasavitsa, dusha-devitsa,
Poliubi zhe ty menia!
Ai-liuli, liuli, ai-liuli, liuli,
Poliubi zhe ty menia !

Literal Translation:
Under the pine tree, under the green tree,
Put (lay) me down to sleep.
Ay, liuli, liuli, ay, liuli liuli,
Put (lay) me down to sleep.

Kalinka, kalinka, kalinka of mine!
In the garden grows a raspberry of mine.
Kalinka, kalinka, kalinka of mine!
In the garden grows a raspberry of mine.

Oh, my beautiful, lovely maiden,
Won't you love me?
Ay, liuli, liuli. Ay, liuli, liuli,
Won't you love me?

Extensions

1. Beth accompanies the song with her mandolin balalaika. The chorus starts slowly then gradually increases its speed, which creates a feeling of excitement and energy.

2. Listen several times to Beth's singing before attempting the words. Join in only on "Kalinka" and "malinka" at first.

3. Sing the chorus of the song with Beth. Older children will gradually be able to join in on the verses.

4. Pat the beat as you sing; use a different body percussion motion to feel the tempo change in the chorus. Clap and stomp together on beats one and three as the chorus gets rolling.

Kalinka

(Snowball Flowers)

1. Pod sos - no - iu, pod ze - le - no - iu, spat' po - lo -
2. Kra - sa - vit - sa, du - sha - de - vit - sia, Po - liu -

zhi - te vy me - nia. Ai - liu - li, liu - li,
bi zhe ty me - nia.

ai - liu - li liu - li, spat' po - lo - zhi - te vy me -
Po - liu - bi zhe ty me -

Chorus
Begin slowly, speed up gradually.

nia! Ka - lin - ka, Ka - lin - ka, Ka - lin - ka mo - ia! Vsa - du
nia!

ia - go - da ma - lin - ka, ma - lin - ka mo - ia! Ka - lin - ka, Ka -

lin - ka, Ka - lin - ka mo - ia! V sa - du ia - go - da ma - lin - ka, ma -

1 *D.C. (Verse 2)*   **2**

lin - ka mo - ia!   Akh - lin - ka mo - ia!!!   HEY!

All about
Malen'kiy Yodzhek

The Hedgehog Song

"**M**alen'kiy Yodzhek" is one of Katya's favorite songs, and very popular with young people in Saransk. She learned it at summer camp when she was about thirteen. A travelling folksinger who was in the area taking part in music festivals came to the camp and taught the campers several songs, stories and singing games. "Malen'kiy Yodzhek" tells of a hedgehog that is very proud of his power. He can carry leaves on his back, or a mushroom, or even a fox, (once he gets over his fears) he is so strong. The words "foofti fu" do not have any particular meaning. It is just hedgehog talk for "Hey, look how great I am!"

Lyrics: (Transliteration)
Málen'kiy yódzhek, chétvero nózhek
Na spiné <u>listók</u> (v. 2: <u>gribók</u>; v. 3: <u>lisu</u>) nesyót
Pésenku poyót, oy!

(Chorus): Foóffti, foóffti, foóffti, fu,
Na spiné listók (v. 2: gribók; v. 3: lisú) nesú
Sámyi síl'nyi ya v lesú,
(1st and 2nd verse): No boyús' odnu lisu.
(3rd verse): Pobedíl samú lisú, foóffti fu.

Translation:
Little hedgehog, four little legs
Is carrying a <u>leaf</u> (v.2: mushroom, v.3: fox) on his back
And is singing a song, oh:

(Chorus): "Fooffti, fooffti, fooffti, fu
I'm carrying a leaf (mushroom, fox) on my back,
I'm the most powerful in the forest,
(Verses 1 and 2): But I'm only afraid of a fox."
(Verse 3): "I conquered even a fox."

Russian Pronunciation

- zh - measure
- a - far
- e - yet
- i - keep
- o - short
- u - flute
- oo - cook
- *Accent marks show emphasis.*

❧ Extensions

1. The children may act out the role of the proud hedgehog, carrying various important things on his back as he struts (in rhythm) through the forest, while they listen to Katya sing the song.

2. Listen a few times to Katya's singing before attempting the words. Say the words in rhythm, then join in on the chorus with "Fooffti, fooffti, fooffti, fu." The verses are actually fairly easy, as they repeat except for the word that describes what the hedgehog is carrying. Older children will gradually be able to join in on the entire chorus as well. Repetition is the key!

3. Learn the following words in Russian and try to use them: (the accent marks show emphasis)
málen'kiy - little
yódzhek - hedgehog
listók - leaf
gribók - mushroom
lisá - fox

Malen'kiy Yodzhek

(The Hedgehog Song)

Ma - lenk'-iy yod - zhek, chet - ve - ro no - zhek

na spi - ne lis - tok nes-yot Pe - sen-ku po - yot, oy!
(2) (gri - bók)
(3) (li - su)

(Chorus):

Fooff- ti, fooff- ti, fooff- ti fu, na spine li - stok ne - su,
(2) (gri - bók)
(3) (li - su)

sam-yi sil'- nyi ya v le - su, *(1&2)* no boy-us' od - nu li -
(3) Po - be - dil sa - mu li -

su. su, fooff- ti fu.

(As sung on the recording by Katya Ponomareva. Transpose if necessary.)

Middle East

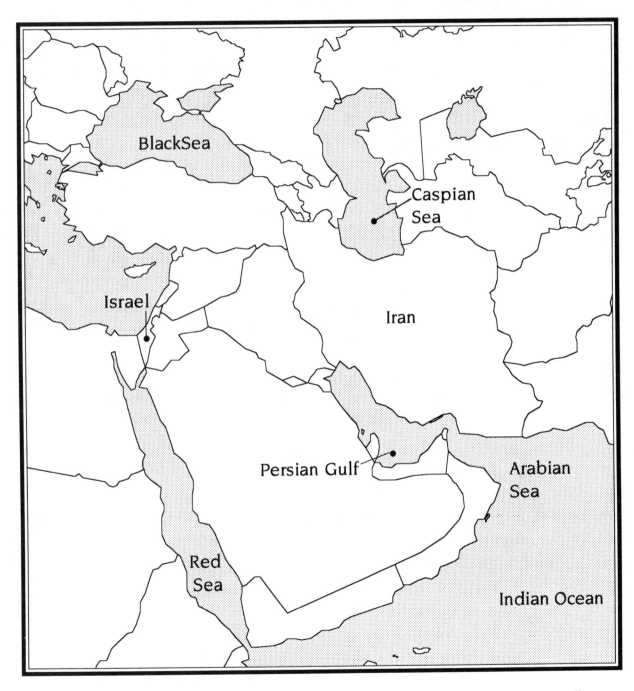

Labels on map: BlackSea, Caspian Sea, Israel, Iran, Persian Gulf, Arabian Sea, Red Sea, Indian Ocean

Iran
Israel

Iran

Mohammad Amirkabirian and his wife Bella

*"My uncle is a famous
Iranian musician,
Jamshid Mohebi.
He is well known for his
performances on the tonbak
or zarb, a goblet-shaped drum.
He made one for me.
I remember his playing it
all the time in my life,
coming to our house
late at night.
He would appear at my
family's door with his instruments
and his friends.
They would perform
in our house for practice
and then play in Teheran."*

- Mohammad Amirkabirian

Mohammad Amirkabirian was born and raised in Tehran, Iran. The United States, where he is studying electrical engineering, has been his home for many years.

Mohammad grew up surrounded by the music of the Persian language itself. Iranian poetry was highly valued by his family, more so than song or dance. He recalls poetry being recited at family gatherings by his parents, two brothers and sister. The Amirkabirian family looked to verse for insight, called *haffoz* in Persian. Mohammad still enjoys listening to and reading Iranian verse.

Mohammad believes in cultural exchange, particularly now that he lives abroad. He and his American wife, Bella observe Iranian holidays all throughout the year. One of their favorites is the Iranian New Year, known as *Now Ruz*. This traditional six-day holiday begins on the first day of Spring. Everyone wears new clothing and uses new dishes. The table is set with a mirror, candelabra, fish, loaf of bread and a green leaf floating in a saucer of water, and also with seven items that start with the fifteenth letter of the Persian alphabet (*sin*). They hold a coin and eat a sweet for luck as the new year is ushered in. On the last Tuesday evening before the Now Ruz begins, Mohammad jumps over a fire to "cleanse the soul." Hopefully the new year will be a good one and any sadness of the old year will depart.

Governed by a string of monarchies until 1979 when the Islamic Republic was ushered in, Iran is a Middle Eastern nation with a long and complex history. Known as Persia until 1935, Iran lies on a high plateau sharing its border with five other nations, including Turkey, Iraq, Afghanistan, Pakistan and Russia. From the shoreline of the Persian Gulf and the Caspian Sea, to the interior desert and rugged volcanic mountains, the terrain is a panorama of contrasts.

Most Iranian people are of Persian descent. Other groups living in the country include the Azerbaijani, Kurds, Luri, Bakhtiari, Baluchi, Arabs, Afghans and Turkomen tribesmen.

Mohammad Amirkabirian as a young child.

Iranians speak Persian, also known as Farsi, and ninety percent are Shiite Muslims. The Shiite women who observe the traditional, orthodox practices completely hide their bodies from public view. Traditionally, therefore, these women will not leave the house unless they are swathed head to toe in a veiled garb known as the *chador*. Some of the less observant women, or those who have become westernized, perhaps by attending college in a non-Muslim country, do not cover themselves in that manner.

The economy of Iran is built primarily upon the oil trade, however Persian caviar and carpets are enjoyed at home and are exported abroad. The exquisite designs and craftsmanship of Persian rugmakers are valued world wide.

The creative imaginings of the Persian poet Omar Khayyam have traveled as well to the far corners of the earth, clinging to the magic carpet of verse. Hafiz (who wrote in the fourteenth century) and Sa'di (of the thirteenth century) are two other beloved

Persian poets. Although their reputation is not an international one, their work is highly acclaimed by Persian speaking people.

The most commonly heard musical instruments include a variety of long-necked lutes, including the *tar* and a long-necked spike fiddle known as the *kemenche*. Wind instruments include the *balaban*, a shawm, similar to an oboe, and a double clarinet called a *duzele*. The *nei* is an end-blown flute. Ubiquitous throughout the Middle East are the goblet-shaped drums known as *dombek* or *zarb*, and zeng, finger cymbals.

Persian nobility - 16th century drawing

All about
Cheshm, Cheshm

Eyes, Eyes

Mohammad learned the chant "Cheshm, Cheshm" from his parents. Most Iranian young children know it, as it provides a fun and easy way to learn how to draw the human body.

Lyrics:
Cheshm, cheshm, doe abru,
Dahmógho, dahan, yay gerdoo,
Chub, chub, shecambé,
Ein augha che gadre gashange!

Translation:
Eyes, eyes, two eyebrows,
One nose, one mouth, one face,
Side, side, one tummy,
What a person—so beautiful!!!

❧ Extensions

1. Listen to the chant and learn the words.

2. Each phrase prompts a drawing of the appropriate body part. One result appears below, for your reference. On the opposite page is a copy master to use with children. The children repeat the chant, then pause to complete that step of the drawing, adding more body parts with each line chanted. When all artists have finished, the masterpieces may be held up and admired, or made into a bulletin board display.

Cheshm, cheshm, doe abru,

Dahmógho, dahan, yay gerdoo,

Chub, chub, shecambé,

Ein augha che gadre gashange!

Cheshm, Cheshm
Eyes, Eyes

Cheshm, cheshm, doe abru,

Dahmógho, dahan, yay gerdoo,

Chub, chub, shecambé,

Ein augha che gadre gashange!

Israel

Rita Klinger and her son

"When I lived in Israel, singing seemed to permeate the culture. Many evenings I gathered with a group of friends, Israelis and non-Israelis, and we would sing for hours accompanied by accordions, recorders, guitars and the ever-present hourglass-shaped dumbek drum."

-Rita Klinger

Rita Klinger's family history is similar to the experience of many of the Jews in the United States. Her mother's parents were Russian and Lithuanian, and had moved to England from Russia. Her mother, born in England, came to the United States after World War II to visit family who had emigrated earlier, and then decided to stay on, and met and married Rita's father. Rita's paternal grandmother was a third generation American of German descent, whose family was among the founders of the Reform Judaism movement in America. Her paternal grandfather was born in Austria-Hungary, and emigrated to New York City at the turn of the century, during a wave of Jewish immigration. Rita was born and raised in New York City, and like many Jewish teens, she was active in Jewish youth groups that sponsored summer programs in Israel. During high school, she spent eight weeks touring Israel and staying on a kibbutz. During that time she fell in love with the country, and developed a strong sense of having arrived home. After studying music education at the Hartt School of Music and teaching vocal music in public school for two years, she returned to Israel to live. During her three years there, she first taught piano and recorder in Bet Shean, a small development town of North African immigrants in the north. For another two years she taught pre-instrumental music in a Jerusalem music conservatory, as well as in a private nursery school for children from preschool through first grade, and sang with the Jerusalem Chamber Choir. She returned to the United States for graduate study, then joined the faculty at Holy Names College as director of the Kodaly summer certification program. She offers workshops on music for children throughout the United States, and includes many children's songs from her years in Israel. She is currently pursuing a doctorate in music education at the University of Washington.

Descended from the ancient Hebrew tribes of the Tigris-Euphrates valley in the Middle East, the Jewish people today live all over the world, but many view Israel as their true homeland. Israel officially became an independent nation in the Middle East in 1948, having originally been the land of Canaan, then Israel, then Palestine. Russian Jews began arriving in

1882. Many more Jews settled in Palestine in the 1930s and '40s, fleeing the devastation in Europe caused by the Nazi Holocaust, seeing it as a safe haven and ancient homeland, in which they might pick up the pieces of their fragmented lives. In 1947, a UN partition plan divided Palestine into two parts, one Arab and one Jewish, keeping Jerusalem as an international city. This plan did not work, and after a civil war, the British gave up the mandate for petition, and Israel was declared a state. Unfortunately, Arab-Jewish conflict and confusion has continued over various areas of land, right to the present. But many Israeli and Arab residents are working together for mutual understanding, striving to live together peacefully in this ancient land.

Israelis whose ancestors have lived in the area for generations live side by side with newly-arrived and returning immigrants from such countries as Morocco, Tunisia, Yemen, Russia, the Ukraine, Spain, the Balkans, Poland, Austria, Germany, France, and the United States. Virtually the entire Ethiopian-Jewish population was recently airlifted into Israel, and is now being resettled, assisted by volunteers.

Much of the desert areas that are now rich agricultural lands were reclaimed from the sands through the hard work of Jewish pioneers living cooperatively in communities called *kibbutzim*. Frontier towns of immigrants seeking refuge and resettlement began to spring up in the 1950s, and today many are thriving communities of ten thousand people or more. In the old cities, ancient structures made of native stone and brick line narrow streets and overlook crowded bazaars. They often stand within view of modern high-rise apartments and office buildings. The streets buzz with a mosaic of mother-tongues, however Hebrew and Arabic are the most widely spoken languages, Yiddish is frequently heard among settlers from Europe, English from the British and Americans, and English is added as a major subject in the schools.

Education begins at an early age for Israeli children, with early childhood centers in cities and government-sponsored kindergartens common throughout the country. Children from two years onward learn to count, read and write, draw, and to interact socially through song and games. In elementary and secondary school, children learn in both English and Hebrew. Even preschools may offer a morning program in Hebrew and an afternoon one in English. Along with the academics, children study music. They sing, play the recorder and pianica, a wind-blown keyboard instrument. They move on to orchestral instruments in the upper grades.

Music plays an important role in unifying the people returned from the Jewish Diaspora to Israel. The Israel Philharmonic Orchestra, the Gadna Israel National Youth Orchestra, and numerous choral groups and chamber ensembles bring people together to perform and to listen to music perceived as culturally without boundaries. The Israeli Composers' League fosters creativity and reinforces a unified Jewish identity. The music of this national school preserves the old even as it embraces the new, and blends Middle Eastern melodies and rhythms with Western harmonies.

National pride is expressed in the popularity of folk music and dance, some of which was composed and choreographed to express the spirit of Israeli nationalism. Popular performers include Geula Gill, Ofra Haza (a Yemenite Jew), and Esther Ofarim, who specializes in music for children. Many children's songs are traditional or composed melodies set to verses by well-known poets Rachel and Bialik. Folk songs are accompanied by the recorder, or shepherd's pipe, accordion (brought from Europe), Middle Eastern *dunbek* (sometimes spelled *dumbek*, or *dunbeki*) finger cymbals, and guitar. Even in the instruments used, one sees the ancient and the modern side by side, as it is in so many facets of Israeli life.

⌐All about
Uga Uga Uga

Cake, Cake, Cake!

Hebrew Pronunciation

- ch = Ba*ch*; h = *h*ead
- g = *g*ood
- a = *a*h
- e = r*e*d; ei = n*ei*gh
- i = m*ee*t
- o = g*o*
- u = cl*ue*
- "ch" is slightly gutteral.

✑ Extensions

Children and their parents all over Israel know "Uga Uga Uga." The melody is traditional, and the words were written by Ashman Aharon. The song is learned by children as young as two years, who will plead "Let's play 'Uga.'" It is as popular in Israel as "Ring Around the Rosy" is in the United States, and is similar at the end with its fall (and rise again). This is the first circle game that most Israeli children play. Rita learned "Uga, Uga, Uga" from children playing in Jerusalem.

Lyrics:
Uga uga uga
Bama-agal na-chuga
Nistoveva kolhayom
Ad asher nimtza makom
Lashevet lakum
Lashavet lakum
Lashavet v' lakum.

Translation:
Cake, cake, cake.
We'll form a circle.
We'll go around all day long
Until we find a place to sit and stand (3x)

1. Learn the Hebrew words. Sit on the word *lashevet* and stand on the word *lakum*. Practice sitting and standing on cue.

2. Chant the words of the song, and then sing the song with Rita.

3. Play the game. Start by forming a circle. Join hands around the circle, sitting and standing three times on the final phrase.

Uga Uga Uga
(Cake, Cake, Cake!)

Words: Ashman Aharon

U - ga u - ga u - ga   Ba-ma agal na-chu - ga

Nis - to - ve - va kol-ha-yom   Ad ash-er nim-tza ma-kom La-

she-vet la-kum   La-she-vet la-kum   La-she-vet v' la-kum.

Melody traditional, lyrics © Ashman Aharon, ACUM, Israel

All about
Yeysh Lanu Tayish

We Have A Goat

"**Y**eysh Lanu Tayish" is a song sung and danced by children in Israel. The opening word, *yeysh*, is rhythmically chanted six times, suggesting the tempo and pulse of the song to singers. The verse describes a goat, and the chorus is simply sung on "la."

Lyrics: (Transliteration)
Yeysh, Yeysh, yeysh, yeysh, yeysh, yeysh.
Yeysh lanu tayish la tayish yeysh zakan
V'lo arba raglayim v'gam zanav k'tan.
La la la....

Translation:
We have, We have, we have...
We have a goat, he has a beard.
He has four legs, and also a little tail.
La, la, la...

❧ Extensions

1. Teach the Hebrew words:
tayish - goat
zakan - beard
raglayim - legs
k'tan - little
zanav - tail

2. As Rita sings the verse, listen for these Hebrew words. Sing along on the chorus.

3. Chant the phrases of the verse in rhythm, then sing both the verse and chorus with Rita.

4. Do the dance steps described below the transcription, clapping in rhythm when partners are not holding hands.

Yeysh Lanu Tayish

(We Have A Goat)

Yeysh! Yeysh! Yeysh, yeysh, yeysh, yeysh, Yeysh la-nu tayish, La

ta-yish yeysh za kan. — V' lo ar-ba rag la-yim, V' gam za-nav k' tan.

La la la la la la La la la La la la la la la

la la la la la la la la la la la la la la la la.

Dance Directions: *(The movements are timed to coordinate with verse and chorus sections.)*
All choose partners and stand in two facing lines.

(Sing): *Yeysh, Yeysh, yeysh, yeysh, yeysh, yeysh:*
(Movement):The head couple holds hands; the others clap in rhythm.

(Sing): *Yeysh lanu tayish, la tayish yeysh zakan:*
(Movement): Head couple gallops sideways down between the lines.

(Sing): *V' lo arba raglayim v' gam zanav k' tan:*
(Movement): Head couple gallops back up between the lines to their original position.

(Sing chorus): *La, la, la etc.:*
(Movement): The head couple forms an arch; all other partners pass under, then separate and
walk rhythmically down the outside of the left and right lines; they rejoin and gallop back up the
middle as partners.
The head couple also separates and goes around the outside down to the end of each line.
The song begins again with a new head couple.

North America

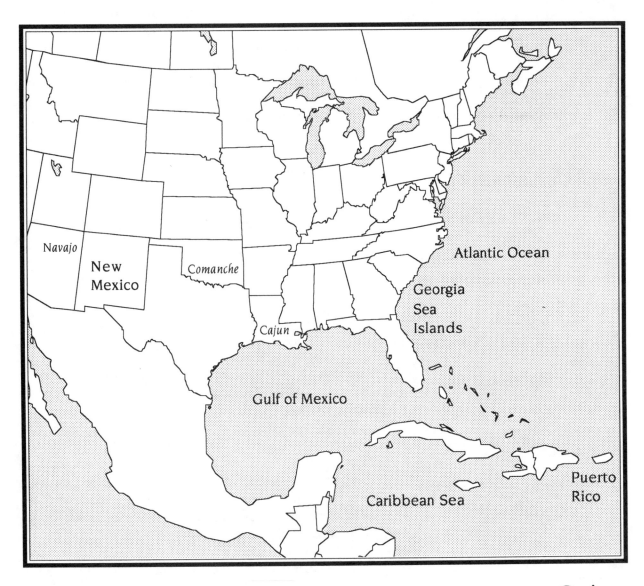

Cajun
Comanche
Georgia Sea Islands
Navajo
New Mexico

Cajun

Jeanie McLerie and Ken Keppeler

"Cajun music developed
as dance music
but it also reflects the feelings
of pain, sorrow and joy
of the people who are Cajuns.
It is a particular kind of music
that you can find
no where else."

- Ken Keppeler

Jeanie McLerie and Ken Keppeler are professional musicians and international performers. Both collect music in the oral tradition, relying on direct personal contact with other traditional musicians to expand their repertoire, and learning new pieces by ear rather than from the printed page. They met while living in Louisiana, where they fell in love with Cajun music and culture (and each other!), and studied intensively there with master folk musicians including Dennis McGee (perhaps the greatest Cajun fiddler), Canray Fontenot, (a Black Cajun fiddler) and Maurice Berzas and Alphonse "Bois Sec" Ardoin (Cajun accordion players). They fully immersed themselves in the music, the food, the language and the community for years, adopting the culture as their own. When Jeanie was advised to move to a dryer climate for health reasons, they chose New Mexico, a return to the southwest for Ken.

Jeanie and Ken are the heart of the New Mexico-based Cajun group Bayou Seco (the group heard here on the companion recording). *Bayou Seco* is a tongue-in-cheek name which means "dry bayou" because, as they laughingly explain, if a swampy bayou existed *at all* in arid New Mexico, it would have to be a dry one! This singing and instrumental group performs the music and dances of New Mexico, French-speaking Louisiana, Appalachia, the southern United States, and the southwestern cowboys. They play diatonic button accordion, fiddle, guitar, banjo, mandolin, harmonica, jawharp, charango and limberjack. They often refer to their performance as "delightfully danceable chile gumbo music." Jeanie has also appeared with the groups Sandy and Jeanie, The Harmony Sisters, and The Delta Sisters. She operates a fiddle school in Albuquerque called "The Fiddler's Friends."

Ken Keppeler is a fourth generation southwesterner, violin maker, and the author of a survey of cowboy music and dance for the Smithsonian Institute. In addition to the accordion, fiddle and mandolin, Ken plays the spoons. He says that the spoons are very practical. You can use them for a musical instrument and eat with them, too!

Jeanie and Ken believe that music is for everybody, and never discourage an aspiring musician.

The phrase *Cajun country* conjures up an image of marshes, swamps, bayous and Cypress trees draped in Spanish moss. Perhaps alligators, horse races, fortunetellers, or even cock fighters come to mind. You might recall the tantalizing aroma of gumbo, crawfish, or turtle soup being prepared. And be sure to add an intimate late night *fais-do-do* or the infectious gaiety of a Mardi Gras celebration.

The portrait would be incomplete without mention of the Cajun people, their expressive French dialect and exuberant music. Put it all together, add a dash of *filé* (fiery hot sauce) and you will have a portrait of bayou life.

The word Cajun is derived from *Acadian*. The Acadians were French-speaking people who settled at Port Royal, Acadia in 1604. In 1713 France ceded Acadia to the British who renamed it Nova Scotia. In 1755, after years of warfare between the British and the French, nearly all the Acadians were expelled from Canada. Their homes and farms were confiscated and families were separated. Many died on ships; others were forced into colonies along the eastern seaboard, and some wound up in the West Indies. By 1764 Acadians were arriving by the thousands in Louisiana. They spread out into the bayous and prairies of southwestern Louisiana and began to establish a life of fishing, trapping and hunting. They carried with them their French language, their love of music and dance, and their fierce family ties. Over time the word "Acadiens" became slurred to form "Cajuns." The area settled by the Cajuns, which was already inhabited by Native American peoples, became a sponge which absorbed immigrants from Europe and the Caribbean, as well as escaped slaves and free blacks (now often referred to as Creoles).

With so many outside influences being absorbed the Cajun language and culture itself took on a new and distinctive flavor. During the early part of the twentieth century this distinctive local identity was threatened with assimilation into the mainstream national culture. Fortunately there were individuals who championed preservation of traditional Cajun ways including their French dialect, storytelling and musical traditions. The late fiddler and National Heritage Fellow Dewey Balfa's stunning debut at the 1964 Newport Folk Festival spurred a revival of Cajun music and a rebirth of Cajun culture.

Cajun fur production leads the nation. The Cajun marshes and swamps are filled with raccoons, muskrats, mink and nutria, an otter-like animal. Another familiar creature in the area is the crawfish. There is a familiar Cajun saying, "Don't crawfish on the deal!" It refers to the crawfish when it is cleaned before cooking. If it accidentally falls out of the cleaning tub, it automatically begins to scoot backwards, away from the tub. In other words, don't back out of a commitment!

The fiddle was one of the earliest Cajun instruments, widely played because it was portable and proved strong enough to survive the rough and tumble bayou life. Fiddlers used double string bowing that created a drone accompaniment and pressed down hard with their violin bows to make their sounds as loud as possible. Singers belted out the melody in high-pitched, nasal tones in order to be heard over the sounds of the fiddlers and dancers. This strong singing style is still common today. Accordions of varying styles (introduced to Louisiana in the mid-1800s by both German immigrants and neighboring Texans), scrub board and a special heavy iron triangle made of hay-rake tines (called *'tit fer*) joined the fiddles and voices to create the traditional Cajun musical sound. Fiddlers were forced to adapt to the strong sound and key limitations of the diatonic accordion—the more genteel fiddle was soon featured primarily on harmony or breaks. Contemporary musicians have added the electric steel guitar and drums. The repertoire is large and varied and includes arrangements of lullabies and children's melodies as well as the ever-present dance songs.

Cajun groups that are well known include the late Balfa Brothers, Beausoleil, Queen Ida, and the "Zydeco King," the late Clifton Chenier. "Zydeco" comes from the French term for beans, *les haricots*, and features driving, repetitive rhythms, often using the piano accordion, and the *frottoir* (corrugated aluminum washboard). In all cases, the rhythms of dance music predominate, and make it hard to sit still when the voices soar and the musicians "let the good times roll."

✍ All about
Bonjour, Mes Amis

Hello, My Friends

❧ Extensions

"Bonjour Mes Amis," which means "hello my friends," is a song used to teach basic French phrases such as *bonjour* (good day!) and *comment ça va?* (How are you?).

Lyrics:
1. Bonjour, mes amis, bonjour
2. Comment ça va, mes amis, comment ça va
3. Ça va bien, mes amis, ça va bien
4. Allons danser, mes amis, allons danser
5. Allons chanter, mes amis, allons chanter
6. Au revoir, mes amis, adieu

Translation:
1. Good day, my friends, good day
2. How are you, my friends, how are you?
3. I'm fine, my friends, I'm fine
4. Let's dance, my friends, let's dance
5. Let's sing, my friends, let's sing.
6. Goodbye, my friends, farewell.

1. Sing the song, paying attention to the French pronunciation and Jeanie's loud, pronounced "street singer" style.

2. Jeanie is playing the six string steel guitar and singing the melody. The accordion is the other background instrument. The accordion embellishes the melody line and the guitar is playing harmonic chords.

3. Identify and clap the prominent rhythmic pattern that occurs throughout the song:

4. Dance the Cajun Two-Step, a "funky" version of a classic ballroom step, while you listen and sing. Everyone has their own way of doing the Two-Step, and every Cajun community has its own distinctive style. Unlike standardized ballroom dancing, the Two-Step has many variations, and lots of room for self-expression. The dancers hold each other in ballroom style with the man leading, or, even more simply, just link arms and walk forward, turn, switch direction—the sky's the limit!

The pattern is:
      step-step-step-pause, step-step-step-pause.
The feet move:
        L-R-L pause, R-L-R pause.

Bonjour, Mes Amis

(Hello My Friends)

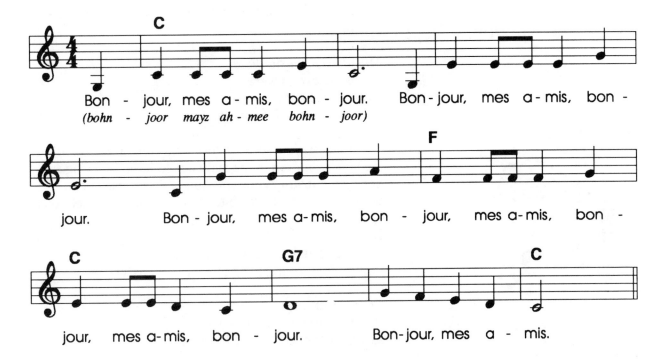

Bon - jour, mes a - mis, bon - jour. Bon - jour, mes a - mis, bon -
(bohn - joor mayz ah - mee bohn - joor)

jour. Bon - jour, mes a-mis, bon - jour, mes a-mis, bon -

jour, mes a-mis, bon - jour. Bon-jour, mes a - mis.

Phonetic pronunciation:
1. Bohn-joor, mayz ahmee, bohn-joor
2. Coh-moh(n) sah vah, mayz amee, coh-moh(n) sah vah
3. Sah vah bee-a(n), mayz amee, sah vah bee-a(n)
4. Ah-lohn dahn-say, mayz amee, ah-lohn dahn-say
5. Ah-lohn chahn-tay, mayz amee, ah-lohn chahn-tay
6. Oh re-vwah, mayz amee, ah-dyuh

All about
Saute, Crapaud!

Jump, Frog!

ᕲ Extensions

"**J**ump, Frog" is a very old Cajun song. The frog population in Louisiana is very "musical." They are well known for their nightly "symphonies" of amphibian sounds. Jeanie describes the froggy chorus like this:

Music here, music there
    music everywhere!
Even on the darkest night,
    There's music in the air!

When Bayou Seco performs this tune they ask all of the small children in the audience to jump like frogs during the instrumental interludes. They also encourage the audience to say "ribbit, ribbit" during these sections.

Lyrics:
Saute, crapaud, ta queve va bruler;
Prends donc courage, un autre va repousser!

Translation:
Jump up frog, your tail must go.
Just be brave, another will grow!

1. Sing along with the recording, paying attention to the French pronunciation. The melody is sung first in French, then in English and back to French again. Jump like frogs during the instrumental interlude and if you want to, say ribbit!

2. Identify the accompanying instruments.

3. Listen as the verses alternate with instrumental sections. Each instrumental section plays the melody and adds a new complementary tune. Listen for the harmony on the fiddle.

4. The tune is simple. The melody line hops up and down like the frog it is describing. The second phrase or musical sentence is the same as the first but lower in pitch.

112

Saute, Crapaud!
(Jump, Frog!)

C ... **G7**

Saute, cra - paud, ta queve va bru - ler; prends
(Sawt crah - poh tah kehv vah broo - lay prahn

C

donc cou - rage, un autre va re - pous - ser! Jump up, frog! Your
dohnk coo - rahj ahn oht vah reh - poo - say)

G7 ... **C**

tail — must go. Just be brave, a - no - ther will grow!

Comanche

Nacona Burgess as a child

"The Comanche
are a very proud people,
often referred to as
'Lords of the Plains.'
All of us need a sense
of cultural pride.
It can keep you happy,
when you think of your ancestors
and have all of those
'bragging rights.'
Keep on being
the best that you can be,
no matter what the time,
date or era."

- Nacona Burgess

Nacona Burgess identifies himself first as *numunu*, a human being, before saying that he is a Comanche. This is in keeping with his spiritual beliefs and the history of the tribe. Virtually all of the Indian nations originally bore names meaning "the people" or "the human beings." The Comanche originally called themselves the "Nerm" meaning "real people."

As a child, he listened to his grandparents and great-grandmother singing traditional songs. His father and maternal grandmother taught him the Comanche style of dancing as well as the ways and beliefs of the Comanche people. His Kiowa/Comanche mother, LaNora, who is a singer, dancer and poet, is descended from a long lineage of chiefs on both sides. She taught him how to make his pow-wow regalia. His family taught him, as they themselves had been taught, to respect the earth, and all living things. Although particulars vary from tribe to tribe, the belief that all living things are interconnected in the Creator's sacred hoop is at the center of traditional Native American spirituality. Nacona grew up with a deep respect for his elders, the earth and his people's traditions. He feels that this respect is missing from society as a whole today.

When he was little, he spent lots of time with his grandparents. They would take him to the pow wows, and he was thrilled when everyone there seemed to know his name. Dancing as soon as he was able to walk, he wore a breech cloth and beads made by his paternal great-grandmother as part of his first regalia.

Nacona is still a frequent participant in pow wow dance competitions, and has won several times. He dances in more than one style.

Nacona is a member of the Comanche *The we kah* or Black Knife Society. Known as the top warriors, this all-male society has special dances which only they perform. Their regalia is adorned with symbols and consists of a black wrap-around cloth and yellow leggings.

Although each has a distinct cultural heritage and traditions, the Kiowa and Comanche tribes share many characteristics as a result of their common homeland and early nomadic lifestyle. Both migrated to the southern plains from the northern part of the United States, making their homes in easy to disassemble and move tipis. Daring equestrian hunters, the men developed an agile and spectacular riding style as they pursued the great buffalo herds. The early Hollywood image of a Plains Indian warrior

or hunter riding bareback and wearing a colorful feathered headdress has erroneously come, in the minds of many people, to represent all Native Americans. Although traditional regalia and headpieces are still worn at ceremonials, festivals and pow wows, contemporary Kiowa and Comanche generally wear conventional western clothing appropriate to their occupation or task at hand in their day to day life.

Southwestern Oklahoma where, today, they share a reservation, has been the home of both tribes since the late 1800s. The Kiowa's original name for themselves was *Kwu'da*, which means "pulling out." But the Comanche called them *Kaigwa*, which means two halves differ, in recognition of the Kiowa warrior hair style which was long on one side of the head and short on the other. Eventually the word "Kiowa" evolved from the Comanche term. "Comanche" came from the Ute expression *Komanticia*, which means "enemy." Pronounced in English, it became Comanche.

From the 1700s to mid-1800s the Kiowa and Comanche thrived and were able to control encroachment of their land by European invaders and other Indian tribes. Horses were so plentiful that it was not

unusual for one Comanche to own several hundred. The Comanche hunted the abundant buffalo putting the entire animal to use. Their way of life was dependent upon the buffalo which provided both food and the material to make shelter, clothing, fuel, weapons and medicine. The Comanche felt so secure at this time that they referred to themselves as "Lords of the Plains."

The mid-1800s marked the end of the old-ways for the Kiowa and the Comanche, who were no longer able to fight the rising tide of settlers from the eastern states and Europe. The settlers brought with them a host of epidemic diseases which killed off hundreds of people and a system of railroads and agriculture which did the same to the buffalo. Times had irrevocably changed.

All, however, was not lost. Possessing a strong oral tradition, the legends and history of the Kiowa and Comanche people survived in the stories, songs and dances which were passed down from generation to generation. These same stories, songs and dances are kept alive today within families, special societies, and at traditional gatherings.

Kima Duinah

I Came Before

A Kiowa Legend

A lonely Kiowa orphan wandered through the woodlands seeking companionship among the animals. One day, he was sitting underneath a beautiful cedar tree when he heard the wind speak to him. The wind told him how to make a flute from the magnificent tree, the instructions for how to take care of it and most importantly, what melodies to perform on it. If he did as he was told, he would win the respect of many, and the heart of the young woman he loved by playing a special song for her on his flute. He copied the sounds of the wind and the trees, and imitated the songs of the birds. As he had been promised, his heartfelt songs gained him the respect and friendship of his people and the love of the woman. He rejoiced when he found happiness through the music of his flute.

The only traditional Native American instruments capable of playing a melody line are the Apache violin (made of the century cactus plant), the Yaqui violin (similar to the European violin), ocarinas, the musical bow and the flute. The flute, which can be traced back to the stone age, is one of the oldest musical instruments in the world. Found in archaeological digs and jazz bands, in chamber ensembles and at pow wows, the flute is a diversified instrument made in a tremendous variety of ways. Flutes might be made of bone, cane, reed, wood, and metals. All flutes do come, however, in one of three basic styles. They are end-blown, side-blown or cross-blown. Historically flutes were used in shamanic ceremonies and for healing and courting, and are often considered symbols for fertility. Flutes are played in many Native American tribes, but it is a particularly strong tradition among the Plains peoples.

"Kima Duinah" is an original work, created and performed for the first time when Nacona was fifteen years old. Like many Comanche flute tunes, it is a "celebrating song" about love and courting. A self-taught musician, he is playing a Comanche flute made by "Doc Tate" Nevaquaya, a famous Comanche flutist and artist. The flute has a whistle-like mouthpiece and four holes in the front and one in the back. The body of the flute is crafted from cedar wood, believed by the Comanche to have spiritual strength and healing properties. Many flutes have a carved wooden bird, bear or other animal that is tied on above the airhole near the mouthpiece, and moves slightly back and forth to tune or clarify the sound.

The Comanche often put cedar in a pouch or bottle and burn it to produce a purifying smoke. When Nacona's father moves into a new house, he smokes or "smudges" cedar in this way and waves a sacred eagle feather to protect their new home.

Extensions

1. The mood of the music is serene and peaceful. What might Nacona have been thinking of when he composed it? Someone he loves?

2. Nacona plays the melody with many embellishments and ornamentation on the notes. The tune starts high in pitch and descends to a lower note, a style typical of much Native American music called a "tumbling strain."

Kima Duinah
(I Came Before)

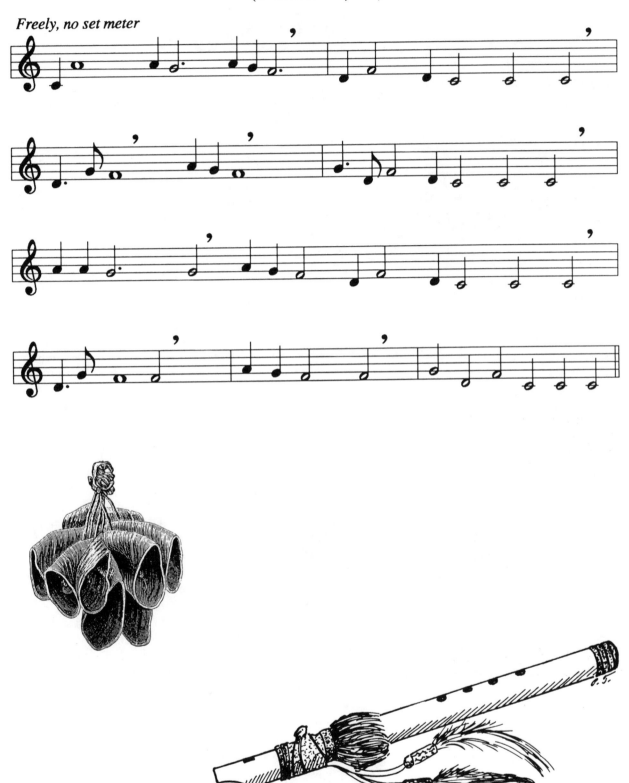

Georgia Sea Islands

Janice Allen performing in the "Summer Revels."

"When I spent time with my family in Georgia, we sang all the time... the old songs, the folk songs, the game songs. And then I heard the stories behind the songs, and about my relatives who sang them. The more I learn about the history and strength of my people from the old songs, the more it empowers and strengthens me to move forward."

- Janice Allen

Janice Allen was born in Philadelphia, Pennsylvania, into a family that loved to sing. Her mother, Jacquelyn Lee Beard, was born in Virginia. Her mother's father, Ulysses Grant Beard, Sr., was of mixed Irish and black heritage, and her mother's mother, Margaret Harris, was half black, half Cherokee. Her father, Richard Allen, was born in Barnswell, South Carolina, son of a Georgia sharecropper Phillip Allen, Sr. and his wife, Maizie Saunders. Life was a struggle for her Georgia grandparents, and times were dangerous—Phillip Allen, Sr. sent his wife north to Philadelphia out of fear of the lynchings that had become common in their area. He himself escaped by secretly riding under a train headed north.

Much of the family remained in Georgia, and Janice remembers how important that tight-knit family was to her during her many visits to their small town in the Savannah area. When she moved to Boston just before first grade and started school, Janice had a strong Southern accent and her speech was peppered with phrases in Gullah, the dialect spoken on the Sea Islands off the coast of Georgia, and picked up by mainland Georgians.

The Allen family homes were filled with music old and new, but always firmly grounded in the African-American culture. Folk songs, singing games, playground chants, Motown, spirituals—all were equally loved. Recipes, too, were a link to the lifeline that had sustained her grandparents' and great-grandparents' generation— dishes like black-eyed peas, pig feet, neck bones, rice, sweet potatoes and chitlins—the throwaways of the white plantation owners that became the sustenance for overworked black bodies and souls. Janice's mother carefully taught the history of the traditions and songs she shared with her six children, as Janice shares now with her own four, and Janice grew up with the understanding that although there were very few books about the real history of her people, a wealth of knowledge was to be found in their music. This was brought home to her even more forcefully when she met and became friends with Bessie Jones ("Miss Bessie"), the late Georgia Sea Islands singer and educator who was an archive of African American music and culture during her lifetime. They performed together in Boston in the "Sea Islands Revels" in the early 1980s, and Janice prepared as her understudy one year when Miss Bessie was not feeling well. Their long personal and professional association had a tremendous impact on Janice, rejuvenating her in her quest for her roots through the meaning imbedded in the music.

After taking part with her siblings in gospel and Freedom Choirs in the black churches and schools during the Civil Rights Movement and after, she knew that her musical ability would become the foundation for her life's work. She received a Bachelor of Music degree from Berklee College of Music, and also earned a diploma from the Kodaly Musical Training Institute. She is currently a music teacher at the Park School in Brookline, Massachusetts, has taught at the Nathan Hale School of Wheelock College and the Boston Children's Museum and numerous other schools, and frequently is called on as a specialist, consultant and performer for radio, television, festivals and conferences. She believes that her work in guiding her students and audiences to a greater understanding of her own and others' cultures will inspire them to look more deeply into their own, leading them to feel more grounded and empowered, and thus contribute in some measure to greater peace in the world.

Some of the strongest retentions of African culture in the United States are found on the lush, low-lying islands that dot the coastline of Georgia and the Carolinas. They include Johns Island, James, Wadmalaw, and Kiawah Islands and others. These islands, like those in the Caribbean, were a first stop for many African slave ships making their way to the North American mainland. Because the Sea Islands' isolation buffered them from urban and white-dominated culture (bridges to the mainland were not constructed until well into the twentieth century in some cases), the deepest roots of African-American culture were largely preserved intact. Blacks working the Sea Islands plantations were under the charge of black overseers for nine months of the year; having no need to camouflage their cultural practices, their unique traditions flourished. The vestiges of African religions blended with Christianity; herbal cures and "charms" were known and practiced by many; songs and dances reflected the structure and nuances of the African musical culture at their core. Their diet was similar in many ways to coastal West Africa—even now, fish, oysters and mussels fill the shallow waters, and the fertile soil and temperate climate produce three crops a year. A regional dialect, Gullah, developed that blended African and English characteristics, and is still spoken today. It is dense with terms that describe the flora and fauna, and is rich with poetic expressions that add color to oral histories.

During the Civil War, the majority of whites fled permanently to the mainland, and the freed blacks formed quiet communities tucked throughout the abandoned plantation lands. However, poverty is still rife in these communities, and the establishment of fancy resorts has raised the value of land and taxes prohibitively for many of the black families who have called the Sea Islands home for generations.

Like African-American music at large, the music of the Sea Islands includes spirituals, blues, call-and-response songs, field hollars, work chants, singing games and stories. Many children's playground songs found even in northern urban areas actually originated in the Sea Islands. Some of the songs include words, phrases, pronunciation or sentence structure with links to Gullah. These lyrics appear simple and straightforward, but closer listening reveals deeper meanings that reflect the inner thoughts of the singer. The Georgia Sea Island Singers, begun in the early 1920s by Lydia Parrish, preserved and shared much of the musical heritage of the islands. One of the best-known of these singers was Bessie Jones (1902-1984), who spent most of her adult years on St. Simons Island. Her rich voice and total dedication to the continuation of the Sea Islands traditions became known to many as she performed as a soloist and also with the Sea Island singers, and recorded and annotated a large body of songs.

Musical techniques evident in these songs include the use of "blue" notes, slurs, slides and vocal percussive elements, as well as body slaps, foot stamps, tambourine and polyrhythmic clapping. Harmonies are most often improvised, and the songs are commonly sung without instrumental accompaniment. The name and repertoire of the Sea Islands Singers is now carried on by Frankie and Doug Quimby, while other singers like Janice Allen also carry the vibrant sounds to eager audiences. The islands' huge oaks, dressed in shawls of dripping Spanish moss, bear witness to the depth and permanence of the Sea Islands culture.

~All about
Uncle Jessie

Janice learned the ring game "Uncle Jessie" on the playground when she was a young child. She also learned a slightly different version from Bessie Jones, (which appears in Miss Bessie's classic collection of African-American children's game songs, *Step It Down*). Uncle Jessie is the boss of the plantation workers. If he has suffered a loss, or if everything is going right, his mood will be reflected in how he deals with the workers. He will step and strut in a show of power. Salt, pepper, onion and garlic refer to the use of herbs and spices as charms to influence someone's behavior. Janice recalls family friends and relatives who frequently mentioned using herbs as charms, and there was a clear understanding that the use of such charms came to them from their African and Native American forebears.

Lyrics:
Now, here comes Uncle Jessie, coming through the field,
With his horse and buggy, and I know just how he feels.

Chorus:
Walk, walk, Uncle Jessie, walk, walk
Walk, Uncle Jessie, walk, walk,
Step, Uncle Jessie, step, step,
Step, Uncle Jessie, step.

Here comes Uncle Jessie, he's looking very sad.
He's lost his cotton and his corn and everything he had.

Now, if you want a sweetheart, I'll tell you what to do,
Just take some salt and pepper and sprinkle it in your shoe.

Now if you want Uncle Jessie to do what you want him to do,
You take some garlic and onion and you put it in his shoe.

❧ Extensions

1. Many cultures have sayings that refer to herbs, spices or other foods and their uses. See how many sayings the children can contribute from memory and also encourage them to ask relatives at home for ideas.

2. This song is very syncopated, as are many African-American songs. Clap or stamp on the off-beat (beats 2 and 4) while you listen to Janice sing. Begin clapping with the chorus.

3. Sing the song and play the ring game, following the directions under the transcription.

Uncle Jessie

1. Now, here comes Un - cle Jes - sie, Com-ing through the field, With his horse and bug - gy and I know just how he feels. Walk, walk, Un - cle Jes - sie, walk, walk, walk, Un - cle Jes - sie walk, walk, Step, Un - cle Jes - sie, step, step, step, Un - cle Jes - sie, step.

2. Now, here comes Un - cle Jes - sie, He's look-ing ve - ry sad. He's lost his cot - ton and his corn and eve - ry - thing he had.

Ring (Circle) Game Directions:

- Form a circle with one person in the center. Those on the outside stand and clap while singing.
- The person in the center broadly mimes Uncle Jessie's actions and attitude while walking rhythmically around the inside of the circle.
- On the last word of the verse, the center person stops in front of someone in the ring, and that person becomes his/her partner.
- Using the skaters hand hold, the partners two-step in the center of the circle during the chorus. Their dance step is sliding, stepping or strutting: **R - L - R - rest, L - R - L - rest.**
- On the last word of the chorus, the old center person goes back into the ring, and the new center person walks inside the circle, acting out the words of the next verse. On the last word of the verse, s/he chooses a partner from the ring and the partners dance as before.
- Repeat for each verse/chorus.

  *Note: Circle games are frequently referred to as "ring" games in the African-American tradition. In these directions, the "ring" refers to the children around the edge, the "circle" refers to the space created by them.

Raggy Levy

"Raggy Levy" is a very old stevedore or dockworkers' song from Georgia. Janice learned this version from Miss Bessie Jones. The song tells of Raggy Levy (or Ragga Levy), a worker who is paid so little and works so hard that his clothes are in tatters—raggedy when he leaves for work and still raggedy when he comes back home. Mr. Sippeli is a secret name used for any slave owner, not necessarily anyone in particular. The stone fence refers to the fact that the slave owner was allowed to barge into the living quarters of his slaves without knocking, ignoring whether they were eating, sleeping, or undressed. No locks were permitted the slaves, and so their fervent hope was to create a private space with a stone fence that would prevent such impositions. The stone fence might also symbolize carving out a different life—one where the individual had a degree of autonomy. Sweet potatoes were one of the survival foods, cousins to the tubers eaten in Africa. Before going to bed, a couple of yams might be put under the coals of the fire, and roasted overnight. The worker would uncover them in the morning, which arrived all too soon. With no time to sit leisurely by the fire, the worker would take them and eat them on the way to work. Reflecting further on a better life, the workers hoped that one day the slave owner might find that everyone had fled to freedom, and there would be no-one left to drive his horse and buggy for free—he'd have to pay a driver, or drive himself. And, finally, Mama Dinah might have been a slave who had gotten too old to continue working well. The slave owner laments that she isn't worth feeding if she can't work hard.

On each "Huh!" and at the end of every other line, the workers would pull together on the heavy rope that hauled the load onto the ship or down from the ship onto the dock, supporting each other's labors by hauling in rhythm, and strengthening each other's spirit by understanding the subtle meaning in the words of their song.

Lyrics:
(Leader): Ah, Ragga Levy,
(Group): Ah-ha, do Ragga Levy (Huh!)
(Leader): Ah, Ragga Levy,
(Group): Oh, boy, well ain't ya raggedy as a jaybird!
(Refrain): (Leader): Ah Mr. Sippili,
(Group): Ha, ha, I'm gwana build me a stone fence.

(L): Ah in a mawnin',
(G): Ah-ha, soon in de mawning (Huh!)
(L): Ah in de mawnin',
(G): When I rise I'm gwana sit by de fiah.
(Refrain)

(L): Ah sweet potata
(G): Ah-ha, sweet potata (Huh!)
(L): Ah sweet potata
(G): Oh boy, I got two in de fiah.
(Refrain)

(L): Y' horse and buggy
(G): Ah-ha, horse and buggy (Huh!)
(L): Your horse and buggy
(G): Oh, boy, there ain't no one ta drive 'em.
(Refrain)

(L): Ah, Mama Dinah
(G): Ah-ha, do Mama Dinah (Huh!)
(L): Ah, Mama Dinah
(G): You too old gal and I can't support ya.
(Refrain)

ꙮ Extensions

1. Grab onto a real or imaginary rope and pull at the appropriate spots. Grunt with the effort of the work.

2. Divide into two groups, or use a solo leader, and sing the lead and group parts in the call-and-response style so typical of work chants.

Raggy Levy

Leader: *Group:*

(Pull) Ah Ragga Le-vy, Ah - ha do Rag-ga Le - vy

Leader: *Group:*

(Pull)
(Huh!) Ah Rag ga Le-vy, Oh, boy, well ain't ya raggedy as a jay bird!

Leader: *Group:*

(Pull) Ah Mis-ter Sip-i-li ha ha, I'm gwan-a build me a stone fence.

Navajo

Marilyn Hood and her children

*"Storytelling,
singing and dancing
are among the fond memories
of my childhood.
My parents would often tell
winter stories
that included traditional songs,
or they would pick me up
off the ground
and perform social songs
and dances with me."*

- Marilyn Hood

Marilyn Hood was born in Fort Defiance Hospital in Arizona and raised in Toh-lah-Kai, New Mexico. Her father's surname was John C. Help. The name was given to the family by European-American neighbors, because her grandfather had a generous spirit and helped others. Their original name was Ts'inajinnie Yidlohigii biye' bitsii' d'goodigii, meaning "Son of the one who streaks across laughing. His hair is cut-off."

She and her five sisters and three brothers were brought up in traditional Navajo ways, speaking Navajo as their first language. When she was a young woman, she was chosen Miss Navajo Nation. (A photo of her wearing her silver crown appears on the cover.)

From her father and grandmother, she learned to weave, as well as how to identify and use the herbs and plants native to the American Southwest to dye fabric.

Like many other Navajo, they lived in a *hogan*, a house made of wood and brick-hard mud. Never square, hogans are round, hexagonal or octagonal in shape, with the door facing east towards the rising sun. They have a central air vent in the ceiling and are warm in winter and cool in summer.

Marilyn still lives in a hogan, near the Navajo Reservation outside Gallup, New Mexico with her five children. They have electricity, but no running water. Marilyn uses her truck to haul water in large containers. The austere beauty of the landscape outside her home has inspired Marilyn's painting in oil and watercolor.

A solo singer and accomplished dancer, Marilyn frequently performs the Two-step and Navajo Skip dances. She teaches her children the traditional songs that she learned in her own childhood. She feels deeply that the old ways should be honored.

The Navajo call themselves Dinéh which means "The People." The largest Native American tribe in the United States, their official home is the large Navajo Reservation, an area that includes parts of northeastern Arizona, northwestern New Mexico and southwestern Utah. Although the climate is arid and rain comes infrequently, the reservation is spectacularly beautiful. Sculpted by nature's own hand, its landscape is one of contrasts: mountains and canyons, buttes, arroyos, and mesas. (A *butte* is a small raised plateau with steep edges. An *arroyo* is a dry riverbed. Large raised plateaus with steep edges are known as mesas.) Local communities bear melodious or evocative names such as Kayenta (named after a spring nearby; the Navajo refer to it with a different word which translates as "water with many fingers"), Chinle (Ch'iinle' in Navajo, meaning "where the water flows out of the canyon"), Shiprock and Crownpoint.

The Dinéh settled in the southwestern part of the United States sometime during the mid-fourteenth century. (Several theories have been suggested regarding where the Navajo had migrated from at that time. The Rockies, Great Basin and High Plains are all possibilities.) For several centuries they have intermingled with other Indian tribes and were influenced by the Pueblos who introduced them to the raising of corn, weaving, and sandpainting ceremonials.

Historically, the American Civil War had a great impact on the Navajo people. After the war broke out many of the garrisons and forts in the southwest were left defenseless as the soldiers stationed there were called east to serve at the front. Seeing an opportunity to possibly regain control of their land, the Navajo and Apache banned together and began to wage war on the settlements. Colonel Kit Carson and his troops staged a campaign to end the attacks.

A relocation policy designed by Captain James Carleton, which ordered the Navajo and Apache incarcerated, was put into effect on July 20, 1863 at Fort Defiance, Arizona. Thus began the forced march known as the "Long Walk" to Fort Sumner, New Mexico. They were detained and forced to remain there from 1864 through 1868. Many died on their trek, and many others during their detention at the fort, where conditions were crowded and unhealthy. On August 12, 1868 a treaty was signed by the Navajo and United States governments and the Navajo were resettled on their 3.5 million acre reservation (160-thousand square miles.) The Navajo Tribal Council which deals with political matters of the Navajo Nation was organized in 1938.

Although some Navajo still raise livestock (especially sheep which provide wool for weaving) and grow crops, the local oil, gas, coal, timber, sand, gravel and mineral extraction industries, as well as retail businesses, provide employment for many members of the Navajo nation. A significant number also live and work off of the reservation in a wide variety of jobs and professions. Navajo schools, the Navajo Community College, and cultural centers teach traditional arts including painting, drawing, weaving, jewelry making, dancing, singing and playing instruments, Navajo language and lore as well as standard academic subjects. Clothing is appropriate to the profession or task, but western style jeans, boots, shirts and hats are very common for men, and the women often wear blouses and skirts patterned after styles of the 1860s. Carved and cast silver and turquoise rings, cuff bracelets, hatbands and belts are worn by men and women, both. A nation of skilled craftspeople, Navajo women are widely known for the beautiful rugs they create and the men for their exquisite silversmithing.

The traditional Navajo society is matrilineal, with the grandmother at the center. All of her children are members of her clan. The mother owns the family dwelling, livestock and crops, tending them with the help of her children. In a traditional family the men and women spend their money independently.

Navajo musical groups frequently play country and western music as well as rock and roll, and sometimes a song in Navajo will be included with English phrases or verses. Attending social dances is a favorite way to spend time off from work or study, during the day or evening, and the dances offer young people a chance to meet and court.

Ceremonies conducted from memory by the traditional singers, shaman, or ceremonial practitioner to restore balance or health to the community or individuals, are an integral part of Navajo life. Those who are empowered to conduct and direct these important rituals have spent years learning every phase of the drama as well as the many chants, beginning as apprentices to recognized practitioners. These rituals might include sandpainting, singing, dancing and prayer, and may be short (an hour or so) or quite lengthy, extending around the clock for several days. When ceremonial singers chant, they will often use special rattles for accompaniment. The ceremonial drum is a water drum made from a clay pot with a buckskin head stretched over the top. It is struck with a twig or thick, flexible branch that has been bent into a loop at the end. Masked dancers representing important spiritual beings participate in some of the healing ceremonies. Life passages are also marked by sacred ceremonies, including coming of age rites for young people about to embark on the lifelong journey of preserving and maintaining the traditions of the Dinéh.

Walking together

Navajo Legend

The earth mother cried and cried
when her son grew up
and left her home.
She was so lonely
that she wept continuously.
Her crying became music
and her son became
one of the Navajo's
famous and glorious heroes.

Noted by John Bierhorst in
A Cry From the Earth

"Jo'ashila," which means "walking together," is a traditional Navajo social song, which Marilyn learned from her father, John C. Help. She accompanies her song by hitting a drum with a padded drum stick. Drums, rattles and scrapers are frequently used by Native Americans to accompany vocal music. The drum Marilyn uses in this piece is not Navajo. (Traditionally only men play the drum for Navajo sacred ceremonies, so it would be inappropriate for a woman to play a Navajo-made ceremonial drum.) The song includes the phrase "hei ya' hei'nee ya" which is made up of vocables, word fragments or syllables that are have no translation but are essential to the expression of the text. Vocables are an integral part of Native American music and expression and, although they are not translatable, should not be interpreted as nonsense sounds. Often a particular emotion or concept is often attached to a vocable and felt by the singer performing the song. The essential Navajo concept of *hozho* (beauty) is expressed by this song—beauty being a state of balance and harmony, not physical attractiveness.

Lyrics:
Jo'ashila Jo'ashila Jo'ashila hei yei' yunga
Jo'ashila Jo'ashila Jo'ashila hei yei' yunga
T'oo ga'nizhonigo bah hozho la
Hei ya' hei' nee ya
T'oo ga'nizhonigo bah hozho la
Hei ya' hei' nee ya
Jo'ashila Jo'ashila Jo'ashila hei yei' yunga
Jo'ashila Jo'ashila Jo'ashila hei yei' yunga
(*Final time, add*: hei yei' yung wei' yunga)

Translation:
Walking together, walking together
Happy about beauty
Walking together, walking together.

Extension

1. Talk about the different types of beauty, and what the children think it means to be beautiful.

2. With one person playing the drum part, try to sing the song with Marilyn. When Marilyn sings she uses a distinctive vocal style which includes a slight amount of tension in her throat.

3. Note the repetition of the vocables "hei yei' yunga" and "hei ya' hei' nee ya." The meter changes several times when these phrases occur.

Jo'ashila
(Walking Together)

34

Jo 'a-shi-lá, Jo – 'a-shi-lá Jo – 'a-shi-lá, hei yei' yun ga.

T'oo ga' ni-zhón-ní-go bah ho-zhó lá hei ya'hei', nee ya. Jo 'a-shi-lá,

Jo – 'a-shi lá, Jo – 'a-shi-lá hei yei' yun-ga. T'oo ga' ni-zhón-ní- go

bah ho-zhó lá hei ya' hei, nee ya. Jo 'a-shi-lá, Jo – 'a-shi-lá

Jo – 'a- shi- lá, hei yei' yung wei' yun – ga.

Dance Instructions:

Perform this simple variant of the Navajo Two-step with this song.

The Navajo women always choose their partners, inasmuch as this is a matrilineal society.

• Partners stand in a circle, with the male on the outside.

• The man holds his right arm up and the woman places her left arm on top (like walking down the aisle in a wedding), or they just join hands, or the woman grabs on to the man's clothing (shirt, jacket, sash, etc.).

• Dancers move in a clockwise direction with the drummer in the center of the circle.

• Start on any foot, moving forward with a slight bounce to the rhythm.

When the dance has ended, the man traditionally gives the woman something as a token of appreciation—a small coin (a penny or dime, for example), or object of clothing (hat, scarf) if he has no small honoring token.

New Mexico

Marie Esquibel as a child.

"My home is often filled with my children and grandchildren, traditional foods, dances and songs. Music is one of the most important things in my life. It is the very essence of my feelings and the way I perceive the world. I cannot imagine life without music."

- Marie Esquibel

Marie Esquibel was raised in Las Vegas, New Mexico. Her grandparents spoke Spanish, and Marie speaks both Spanish and English. Some of her fondest memories are of the traditional Spanish foods made by her grandmothers, especially *bizcochitos*, traditional holiday cookies made with anise and cloves that are cut into bite-sized shapes, especially diamonds, circles and triangles, and popped into the mouth. Hymns were sung in Spanish during services at the Presbyterian Church her family attended, and these form some of her earliest musical recollections.

Both sides of Marie's family trace their roots to Spain. Her maternal grandfather came to the United States from Spain, and her ancestors on her father's side came from Spain and settled in New Mexico several generations ago, in Chacón. Members of her family have lived primarily in northern New Mexico.

Marie was raised in a secure and safe environment, enveloped in the warm love of her family and surrounded by beautiful music. Marie's mother loved music, and encouraged Marie and her brother and two sisters to learn music and dancing. She began studying piano at eight years old. At fourteen, she was already the leader of a church choir.

Perhaps as a way to connect more strongly with her heritage, she became a music teacher in the public schools of New Mexico, and over time, delved deeply into the treasury of Spanish songs and dances found throughout the state. Her long search brought her to co-author a book and tape, *Music of New Mexico to Dance and to Sing*. When she shared her collection with her parents and in-laws they were surprised and gratified—she had rediscovered many of the half-forgotten songs and dances of their own childhood. Marie is now teaching her grandchildren the traditional Spanish songs of New Mexico.

So beautiful it casts a spell over visitors and natives alike, New Mexico's state nickname is "The Land of Enchantment." Although it is frequently referred to as a tri-cultural community of Native, Hispanic and European Americans, many other groups live in the state as well, contributing to its dynamic blend of music, myth and customs.

This rugged plateau that is home to both the Sangre de Cristo Mountains and the Rio Grande was also home to the Pueblo people—the original inhabitants encountered and named Pueblo by the Spanish explorers after their style of congregate dwellings and their villages. Made from a special mixture of sands, clays, lime, sticks and water, the adobe building material hardened in the desert sun to become an excellent insulator from both heat and cold. With judicious patching of spots that might have deteriorated due to the action of wind and water, these ancient apartment houses survived in many locations, including on mountain cliffs, and are still in use today, in some cases by descendants of families of 500 years ago! (There are now nineteen pueblos in New Mexico, including Zuni, Santa Clara, Taos and Acoma.) Zuni included a seven-story structure that gave rise to the legend of the "Seven Cities of Cibola," when one of the early explorers reported that he saw the sun reflected from buildings of gold. Coronado's expedition sought this golden city at Zuni. Much to his disappointment, closer inspection revealed the mud buildings had mica flecks that reflected the sunlight!

Finding no gold, the Spanish explorers laid claim to the land itself and sent missionaries to convert the indigenous people to Catholicism. Over time, the missions were withdrawn, because most of the Zuni people would not give up their traditional ways. Some did convert, and adopted many Spanish customs; some combined elements of the new Catholic religion with their traditional beliefs. Exploration and settlement continued and the area became a province of the Spanish colony of Mexico in 1609. After Mexican independence in 1821, it remained a Mexican province. Traders moved through the area coming from Missouri via the Santa Fe trail, and the US official presence began in earnest during the Mexican War in 1846. By 1850, the Territory of New Mexico had been organized. It become a state in 1912.

The Spanish people have made a rich contribution of folk tales and legends to the culture of New Mexico. Many New Mexican children grow up familiar with the Spanish legend of La Llorona. La Llorona, the story goes, was a beautiful lady who had the great misfortune to lose her husband and children. Because her soul is still so lonely, she appears as a ghost wandering around at night looking for little ones to replace her own son and daughter. Children of New Mexico hear that if they sneak outside to play in the late evening, or willfully stay awake when it's time to sleep, there is a chance that La Llorona may catch them.

Many of the early Spanish settlers were sheep-herders or farmers. Caring for sheep  requires extended periods of sitting still, yet remaining alert to watch over the flock. Many songs and pastimes were created to fend off boredom and sleep. "Veinte y Tres" (Twenty Three), for example, is a musical gambling game. One shepherd sings the song while another marks a line with a stick on the ground, keeping track of the number of beats in the song. If the contestant has marked twenty-three, he wins.

A familiar Spanish children's song, "Don Gato," is a good example of a romance or ballad, a song that tells a story. This tune is quite old and its roots can be traced back to Spain. It describes a tomcat who is in love with a gorgeous female. When she writes him a romantic letter he falls off the roof of the house he is sitting on and dies. But since a cat has nine lives, the aroma of fish from a nearby market bring him back to life.

Many Spanish song forms, such as the *romance*, *décima*, and *canción* are over four hundred years old. They are still sung in New Mexico today, as well as more recently developed forms such as the *corrido*. A *décima* is a ten-line verse with melody. *Canción* means song. Ballads which describe historical events, a hero, politics or everyday people and events are known as *corridos*. These song forms are typically accompanied by guitar. Some of the individual ballads are very old songs with roots in Spain, including the well-known ballad of El Cid, the Spanish hero who fought the Moors in the eleventh century.

Clearly, New Mexicans have strong connections to the past as they keep it alive in the present.

All about San Sereni

"San Sereni" is a song that mimes traditional occupations, common many years ago, among early settlers in Latin American countries, as well as the United States. Other versions of the song are popular in Mexico and Puerto Rico. "San Sereni" is a favorite with Marie's kindergarten through fifth grade students at La Mesa Elementary School.

Lyrics:
San Sereni de la buena, buena vida,
Hacen así, así (los zapateros)*
Así, así, así,
Así me gusta a mí.

*Las bailadoras
Los carpenteros
Las pianistas
Los campañeros
Las costureras

Translation:
San Sereni of the good, good life.
(The shoemakers)* do like this.
I like it this way!

the folk dancers
the carpenters
the pianists
the bell-ringers
the seamstresses

~ Extensions

1. Learn the Spanish words for the various occupations.

2. The words and melody are repeated. Only one word changes in each verse - the occupation.

3. The nylon-string guitar and acoustic string bass accompany the soprano singer, with an instrumental interlude between each verse. The guitarist plays the melody during the instrumental sections with a harmony in thirds. This is a typical Latin American harmonic structure.

4. Sing and move to the beat, feeling the strong and weak beats.

5. Make appropriate gestures for the shoemakers, folk dancers, carpenters, pianists, bell-ringers and seamstresses in the song. Which of these occupations are still practiced today? Make up gestures for contemporary occupations.

6. Compare to similar singing games, such as "This is the Way We Wash Our Clothes."

San Serení

San Se - re - ní de la bue-na, bue-na vi - da,
(sahn seh - reh - nee day lah buay- nah, buay- nah vee - dah

ha - cen a - sí, a - sí los za - pa - te - ros, a -
ah - sehn ah - see ah - see lohs zah - pah - tey - rohs ah -

sí, a - sí, a - sí, a - sí me gus - ta a mí!
see ah - see ah - see ah - see mey goos - tah mee)

Singing game instructions:

1. Select a pantomime leader for each occupation in the song.

2. Stand in a circle throughout, or form a circle and walk to the left. When the word *así* is sung, the pantomime leader acts out the occupation, and the group then mimics the leader as each occupation comes around in turn. Movements should be to the beat of the song. Continue each pantomime during the instrumental interlude.

3. Start the new motion with each new verse.

South America

Caribbean Sea

North Atlantic Ocean

Ecuador

Brazil

South Pacific Ocean

South Atlantic Ocean

Brazil
Ecuador

Brazil

Orlânia Freire with her family

*"What is Brazil to me,
if not the sunny beaches,
the agua de coco verde de praia
(coconut juice), Carnaval,
and the samba?
We Brazilians like to dance,
and the rhythms of music
are in our blood."*

- Orlânia Freire

Orlânia Freire was born and raised in the city of Teresina, in the northeastern region of Brazil. She was the oldest girl of eight children, all of whom studied piano, violin or guitar. Her mother was her first piano teacher, after which she studied with private teachers. She vividly recalls the music of Natal (Christmas), Pastoril, and Carnaval, when she would sing carols or songs, and dance with other children and adults in celebration of the season. Her large family would line up alongside each other in the pews at church on Sunday mornings, and sing traditional Roman Catholic hymns in Latin and Portuguese.

In college, she pursued a degree in law, but soon after completing her internship in Rio, left law and Rio behind, choosing instead to study music at the Conservatorio de Musica Alberto Nepomuceno in Fortaleza. There she received a piano certificate, and took courses that would license her to teach music in the secondary schools. She fulfilled her dream to create a private school for music instruction when she returned home to found and direct the Escola de Arte de Teresina. She taught piano and flute, and hired others to teach guitar, dance and painting. After receiving a master's degree in music at the University of Iowa, she returned to Brazil, to a faculty position in music at the University of Piaui in Teresina. Currently she is working on a text for the teaching of Brazilian children's songs to Brazilian teachers and their students.

Brazil is the fifth largest country in the world. Its land covers almost half the continent of South America, and forms the boundary of every country except Chile and Ecuador! Brazil is divided geographically into four large regions: a long band of coastal lands running north to south along the Atlantic Ocean; the enormous central plateau with its western Mato Grosso grasslands; the forested Amazon River basin in the north; and the Paraguay basin in the south, with open forest and scrublands. Beyond the large cities such as Rio de Janeiro and Sao Paulo, much of Brazil is sparsely populated. Most of the Mato Grosso and Amazon regions were explored by Europeans only during this century, with discoveries still being made

Brazil's economy is peppered by agricultural and mineral development. Sugar cane, coffee, bananas, and coconuts are among the exported foods, and oil deposits in the Amazon and off the coast of Rio de Janeiro are the richest reserves in the world. Unemployment is rampant, however, and Brazil's poverty level is similar to the poorest countries in Africa and Asia.

Portuguese expeditions landing on the coast of Brazil in the early 1500s found indigenous hunter-gatherers and fishermen living in small groups. Many more of the approximately four million native people lived in the wetlands of the interior; today, however, there are less than 200,000 descendents of the original inhabitants. The Portuguese colonized Brazil, establishing large plantations served first by native people, and later by large numbers of Africans who were brought to Brazil from Angola, the Congo, Nigeria, and Dahomey over a period of over three hundred years.

Intermarriage among the Portuguese, Indians and African slaves was common from the earliest years of colonization, and gradually the three races became thoroughly blended. As a matter of fact, Brazil has the most racially blended population of South America. By the late nineteenth century, many Europeans from Italy, Portugal, Spain, Germany, and Russia came to work on the plantations. Beginning in 1908, Japanese immigrants also joined the work force, gradually creating the largest Japanese community outside of Japan, in Sao Paulo. Now one of the most populous countries in the world, 75% of Brazil's population of over 123 million is concentrated in the cities.

The largest Catholic population in the world is said to reside in Brazil, but Brazilian Catholicism is noted for its diversity. The religious practices of African slaves were fused with Catholic ritual, and African gods, called *orixas*, were assimilated with Catholic saints, resulting in the development of unique cultural/religious sects such as Candomble and Macumba. These Afro-Brazilian religious traditions integrate music and dance in many of their ceremonies and celebrations.

Folk, traditional, and popular music in Brazil also reflects the country's diversity.

Portuguese and Spanish-styled harmonies, and Portuguese melodies abound, particularly in the children's songs. Stringed instruments such as the *viola*, a five-string double-course guitar, and the *rabeca*, or fiddle, are direct descendents of instruments from old Portugal. Various drums and other percussion  instruments, including the beaded calabash called *afoxe*, wooden scraper known as *reco-reco*, and wooden xylophones derive from West Africa. The African legacy is also clear in call-and-response singing, the use of syncopation and cross-rhythms, and the abundance of melodies with flatted seventh degrees. Knowledge of indigenous music is less known, although rattles similar to maracas are present in Brazilian music.

Brazilian culture resides strongly in the many festivals and folk events throughout the year, most of them associated with religious feasts. Natal, or Christmas, is a time for family gatherings, dinners, gift-giving, and the singing of carols. Pastoril, in early January, commemorates the worship of the new-born Christ-child by the three kings, and the massacre of the holy innocents by King Herod. At Pastoril, small groups of singers (usually girls dressed in blue and white or red and white dresses), travel from house to house, singing, dancing and playing the tambourine. There are other celebrations that highlight Brazilian culture, but none is as sweeping as the pre-Lenten Carnaval, or Mardi Gras—the non-stop, three-day, high-energy extravaganza that begins with feasting, singing, and dancing in clubs and samba schools, and spills out into the streets in raucously colorful parades. The samba is the Brazilian national dance, and huge samba bands show off their choreography, musical arrangements and brilliant costumes imaginatively crafted with feathers, sequins and towering, elaborate headdresses as they strut through crowded streets.

Serra, Serra Serrador

Saw, Saw Lumberjack

Portuguese Pronunciation

- "a" = f*a*r,

- "e" = h*ey*, or m*ee*t

- "i" = m*ee*t, "o" = b*oo* or g*o*
- "u" = *oo* (before), *oh* (after) a word

- "s" before o = z; at end of word = sh

- "z" = mea*s*ure

🙿 Extensions

"**S**erra, Serra, Serrador" is a counting song well-known in Teresina. It is typically sung by mothers or grandmothers to their infants and young children. Orlânia remembers her grandmother singing it with her; later, she sang it to Sergio, her own son. While singing, Orlânia sits in a chair, with the child facing her on her lap. (In a school or daycare setting, the child may sit across from the adult.) She holds the child's hands and rocks and sways to the beat. The text describes the sawing of wood, and the question of how many pieces sawn is answered by counting up to any number.

Lyrics:
Serra, serra serrador,
Quantos paus o senhor serrou?

Um, dois, tres, quatro, cinco, seis, sete, oito, nove, dez.

Translation:
Saw, saw, lumberjack,
How many pieces of wood do you saw, sir?

One, two, three, four, five, six, seven, eight, nine, ten.

1. Gently sway back and forth while listening to the song. Children will enjoy holding their favorite stuffed animal or doll and rocking them in their laps.

2. Say "Quantos paus o senhor serrou" after hearing it sung. Chant it rhythmically, then sing it. Count to ten in Portuguese, using call-and-response at first to assist the children. Count numbers of blocks, fingers, desks, chairs etc. to engage the children in using the Portuguese numbers in day-to-day activities.

3. Follow the rise and fall of the melody with the hands, trace the higher and lower pitches in the air, or draw them on paper or on the blackboard.

Serra, Serra Serrador

Saw, Saw, Lumberjack

Ser - ra, ser - ra ser - ra - dor. Quan - tos

paus o se - nhor ser - rou?

(Spoken): Um, dois, tres, quatro
cinco, seis, sete, oito,
nove, dez!

Dona Maricota

Dona Maricota

"**D**ona Maricota" is a favorite circle game of young Brazilian children. Orlânia learned the game from her neighborhood friends when she was about six years old, by listening and watching them, and finally joining in. The origin of the gamesong is unknown, but *dona* usually designates a married woman and *Maricota* is a nickname for Mary (*cota* being an address of endearment added to the name of a close friend).

Lyrics:
(Group): Dona Maricota,
Como tem passado?
(solo): Por onde eu tenho ondado,
Tenho passado muito bem.
Melhor eu passaria se vôce fosse meu bem.

Translation:
(Group): Dona Maricota
How are you doing?

(Solo): The places I have been,
I have had a good time.
But I would have a better time if you were with me.

✿ Extensions

1. Practice saying "Como tem passado," incorporating it in a conversation. Note that *dona* is a Portuguese address for a woman, but *seu* precedes a man's name in Brazil.

2. Sing the question posed by the group in Portuguese (*Dona Maricota, como tem passado?*), then invite children to create their own responses to the question, singing in English to the existing melody.

3. Listen for the group and solo parts of the song. They differ in that the pitches of the group's melody moves in skips, outlining a chord; the solo melody moves stepwise from high to low.

4. Sing first the group and then the solo parts of the song. Next, choose small groups or soloists to sing individual phrases or the entire solo part.

5. Play the game. The child chosen to be "It" will move into the middle of the circle, and should be encouraged to sing the solo part loudly and clearly.

Dona Maricota

Do - na Ma - ri - co - ta,   co - mo tem pas - sa - do?   Por
[doh - nah mah - ree - coh - tah   coh - moh tay(m) pah - sah - doh   pohr

on - de eu te - nho en - da - do tenho pas - sa - do mui - to bem.   Me -
ohn - joo   tay - noon   dah - doh tay(n)oo pah - sah - doh mooee - too bay(m)   mee -

lhor eu pas - sa - ri - a se vo - cê fos - se meu bem.
oo reeoo pah - sah - ree - ah see voo - say   foh - see meeoo bay(m)]

Directions:

• Children form a circle around one child, who is "It."

• As the singing begins, the child in the center steps to the beat around the inside of the circle, pointing to each child as he/she passes.

• On the very last word, "bem," "It" freezes and points to the nearest child, who becomes the next "It."

Ecuador

Elizabeth Villarreal Brennan

"My father taught me to listen - to the songs and stories of Ecuador, and to the wind. He said that if we listened very carefully, we would hear the wind singing. And if we could hear it singing, we would learn to truly see."

- Elizabeth Villarreal Brennan

The daughter of a professional storyteller, Elizabeth Villarreal Brennan was born and raised in Ecuador. As a child, she and her family travelled with her father as he toured Ecuador's cities and villages telling tales. Her father was Incan and spoke Quechua as his first language. He was raised in the *altiplano* (high plains) region of Imbabura Province. The *altiplano* is an agricultural and cattle ranching area, known for its beautiful lakes and mountains. Her mother, a *mestizo* of mixed Spanish and indigenous ancestry, came from the coastal city of Guayaquil.

One of four girls and three boys in a musical family, Elizabeth was never without other musicians to sing and play with. When she was just six years old, she and her sisters performed traditional Ecuadoran songs and dances on radio, TV, and in theatres. Their ensemble was called "Hermanas Villareal."

At the age of 15, she joined the "Jacinto Jaramillo Folklore Company," and performed songs and dances of both Columbia and Ecuador. She appeared regularly with them on the "Apuntes Sobre el Folklore" program televised in Bogata, Columbia. As a young adult, she and one of her sisters re-established "Hermanas Villareal" as a duet, and toured South America performing and recording the beautiful music of the Andes Mountains.

In the early 1970s Elizabeth came to New York where she earned her certification in Orff-Schulwerk. She headed the bi-lingual Orff program for the New York City public schools and directed the musical summer camp at the Bloomingdale House of Music. In 1988, her book and tape *"A Singing Wind: Five Melodies from Ecuador"* was published. Currently teaching at the Settlement Music School in Philadelphia, she is a frequent presenter of workshops on music and customs of Ecuador.

Land of penguins and panpipes, snow-covered Andean peaks and steamy Amazonian rainforest, Ecuador is a nation of contrasts. Peopled by descendents of the ancient Incan empire as well as Spanish conquistadors, even its location reflects a certain duality. Bisected by the equator, part of this small nation is situated in the northern hemisphere and part in the southern hemisphere. *Ecuador* means equator. The mainland is made up of three distinct regions: *Sierra*—lofty Andean mountain highlands; *Costa*—densely tropical coastal lowlands; and

Oriente—steamy eastern, Amazon river basin rainforests. Ecuador's fourth region is the Galapagos Islands, which lie 600 miles west of Ecuador's coast.

Once known primarily as an exporter of bananas, shrimp, coffee, and the grasses used to make Panama hats, Ecuador's most important product today is petroleum. The discovery of oil in the 1970s has not had much effect on most of Ecuador's people. Much of the rural population still live in traditional ways, unaffected by economic change in urban areas such as Quito, the capital city, or Guayaquil.

With a population as diverse as the terrain, 80% of Ecuador's people have indigenous ancestry. Many describe themselves as "Los Indígenas" rather than "Indians," (a term which some regard as an insult). This group includes the Otavalo people of the highlands. About half the indígenas are *mestizos*, of mixed indigenous and Spanish extraction. The Jivaro people are hunters and fishers and inhabit the tropical forests. Of the remaining population, half are the descendents of African slaves brought to Ecuador during its colonial days. The others trace their ancestry to the Spaniards who ruled Ecuador for more than four hundred years starting in the 1500s.

A quarter of a century prior to Spanish colonization, Ecuador had been absorbed into the powerful Incan empire. The Incas imposed Quechua, the language of their dominant tribe, on all the peoples in their empire. Today Spanish is spoken throughout Ecuador, although most indigenous people are bilingual, speaking Quechua as their mother tongue.

Traditional culture has been preserved in festivals, many of them celebrations of the feast days of the Roman Catholic liturgical year. Pre-Christian agrarian celebrations and customs have been adopted into the observation of church holidays. Carnival, the gala season just prior to the solemnity of Lent, is the occasion for water fights as well as fruit and flower festivals. Easter is observed with dramatic street processions. The ancient harvest fiestas are preserved in the Corpus-Christi festivals of early June. All Souls' Day is observed by flower-laying ceremonies in the cemeteries. Christmas and New Year's are the occasion for parades and street dances.

Ecuador's rich potpourri of indigenous, Spanish and African cultures has simmered to produce a unique musical blend. With a repertoire of religious, work, and lively dance-songs accompanied by drums, the music of the Andean highlands most often features indigenous as well as *mestizo* forms and instruments. Most of the melodies contain short, repeated patterns and phrases. The Spanish influence is heard in lullabies, children's play songs and religious music as well as the *pasillo*, a waltz-like dance. Along the coast, African-derived marimbas, drums and rattles accompany singing or dancing. *Los Indígenas* maintain their distinctive heritage playing panpipes, the rounded single-set of bamboo pipes called *rondador*, *kena (*or *quena)* and *pingullo* flutes made of reeds, wood, clay or even bone, as well as small *tambor* and large *bomba* drums. Maracas called *chil-chil* are made of dried gourds with beans or small stones inside; other shakers are made from bone, clay, shell and found metal pieces. These indigenous woodwinds, drums and percussion instruments are frequently heard along with guitars and *charangos*, the small ten stringed guitar with a body made of an armadillo shell. For a brief period, during Ecuador's colonial days, native Ecuadorans were not allowed to play Spanish-style instruments, such as the guitar. A popular bit of folklore holds that the guitar-like *charango*, small enough to be quickly concealed beneath a poncho, was developed by indigenous people who wished to circumvent this law.

In the market place, traditional and contemporary clothing styles and customs mingle. Indigenous families bring their woven goods, pottery and foods to sell. The women might dress in brightly colored full skirts, intricately embroidered blouses, women woolen shawls in bright patterns, loomed belts in brilliant hues and to top it off, a bowler or derby felt hat. It is common to see men in jeans, cotton shirts, leather or denim jackets and work shoes, but they might also wear loose shirts with embroidery, woven sashes and belts, and loose pants with sandals. Ecuadorians who are not *los indígenas* wear western-style business or work clothes appropriate to their activities.

The soul of the Andes and the spirit of the people echoes in the breathy timbre of the panpipes, in the strumming patterns of the charangos and guitars. Infectiously joyful or searingly moody, the music transports listeners, if only in imagination, to the soaring, enchanted mountains of Ecuador.

ꕥAll about
El Juego Chirimbolo

The "Chirimbolo" Game

ꕥ Extensions

"**E**l Juego Chirimbolo" is a singing game played by young children in Ecuador. Like "hokey pokey," "chirimbolo" is a sound that cannot be translated, but children enjoy saying it. (Literally, it refers to some sort of contraption.) The parts of the body used to play the game are named in the song. The singing and movements of "El Juego Chirimbolo" become more game-like as the tempo increases. The object is to maintain the movements at ever-faster speeds, without becoming confused, distracted or "falling apart."

Lyrics:
El juego chirimbolo, que bonito es,
Con el pie, otro pie,
Una mano, otro mano,
Un codo, otro codo.

El juego chirimbolo, que bonito es,
Con el pie, otro pie,
Una mano, otro mano,
Un codo, otro codo.
El juego chirimbolo, que bonito es, ¡Hey!

Translation:
The Chirimbolo game, how beautiful it is
With your right foot, your left foot,
Your right hand, your left hand,
Your right elbow, your left elbow.

(repeat)

1. "Que bonito es" is literally translated as "how beautiful it is." The expression is used in the same way people in the United States say "beautiful!" in place of "terrific" or "cool" to describe something good, fun, or satisfying. Chant the phrase rhythmically. Think of situations when it might be used;
Delicious ice cream - *Que bonito es!*
Your team wins at baseball - *Que bonito es!*
School's out for vacation - *Que bonito es!*

2. Introduce the spanish words for foot (*pie*), hand (*mano*), and elbow (*codo*). Play a game of "Simon Says" substituting the Spanish words (e.g. "Simon says touch your *mano*.")

3. Sing the song. Listen for the repeated melodic pattern (mi-sol) and its variations.

4. When everyone is comfortable with the song, play the game. (See directions under the transcription)

El Juego Chirimbolo

(The "Chirimbolo" Game)

El (el) jue-go (huay-goh) chir-im-bo-lo (cheer-ihm-boh-loh), que (kay) bo-ni-to (boh-nee-toh)

es (ehs), con (cohn) un (oon) pie (peeay), o-tro (oh-troh) pie (peeay), u-na (oo-nah) ma-no (mah-noh), o-tra (oh-trah)

ma-no (mah-noh), un (oon) co-do (coh-doh), o-tro (oh-troh) co-do (coh-doh). El (ehl) co-do (coh-doh), ¡El (ehl)

jue-go (huay-goh) chir-im-bo-lo (cheer-ihm-boh-loh), que (kay) bo-ni-to (boh-nee-toh) es! (ehs) ¡Hey!

Game directions:

Form two lines facing each other and hold hands with the person directly across from you.

1. *El juego chirimbolo, que bonito es:* while holding hands, take four open-close steps sideways beginning with the left foot: left-close, left-close, left-close, left-close

2. *Con un pie:* extend right foot toward partner, touching outside of partners' extended foot, tap floor

3. *Otro pie:* repeat, using left foot

4. *Una mano, otra mano:* partners clap right hands across, then left hands across

5. *Un codo, otro codo:* partners touch right elbows across, then left elbows across

6. *El juego chirimbolo, que bonito es:* take four open-close steps beginning with right foot this time

7. Repeat entire sequence, steps 1-5 above, beginning instead with the left foot, left hand, left elbow

8. After second ending: *El juego chirimbolo:* partners hold hands, take two open-close steps sideways beginning with the left foot. On *que bonito es:* partners raise hands over heads and make one quick complete turn to the left. On *Hey!:* partners drop hands, jump up, fling arms into the air with fingers extended and freeze.

Selected Bibliography

(* Titles with an asterisk indicate book and audio recording sets)

*Abrahams, Roger D. and Lois Rankin, *Counting-Out Rhymes. A Dictionary.* (Austin TX, University of Texas Press for the American Folklore Society, 1980)

*Adzenyah, Abraham Kobina, Dumisani Maraire and Judith Cook Tucker, *Let Your Voice Be Heard: Songs from Ghana and Zimbabwe* (Danbury CT, World Music Press, 1986)

*Amidon, Peter and Mary Alice, *Jump Jim Joe: Great Singing Games for Children* (Brattleboro VT, New England Dancing Masters, 1991)

*Amidon, Peter, Mary Cay Brass and Andy Davis, *Chimes of Dunkirk: Great Dances for Children* (Brattleboro VT, New England Dancing Masters Productions, 1991)

*Amoaku, W. Komla, *African Songs and Rhythms for Children* (New York, Schott, 1986)

*Bellber, William and Marta Montañez, arr. and eds., *Canciones de mi Isla: Songs of My Island (Puerto Rico)* (New York, ARTS, Inc. 1981)

*Bierhorst, John, *A Cry From the Earth: Music of the North American Indians* (Santa Fe, Ancient City Press, 1979)

*Brennan, Elizabeth Villarreal, *A Singing Wind: Five Melodies from Ecuador* (Danbury CT, World Music Press, 1988)

Bronner, Simon J., *American Children's Folklore: A Book of Rhymes, Games, Jokes, Stories, Secret Languages, Beliefs and Camp Legends* (Little Rock AR, August House, 1988)

*Burton, Bryan, *Moving Within the Circle: Contemporary Native American Music and Dance* (Danbury CT, World Music Press, 1993)

Chase, Richard, *American Folk Tales and Songs* (New York, Dover, 1971)

*East, Helen, *The Singing Sack: Twenty-eight Song-Stories from Around the World* (London, A & C Black, 1989)

Ebinger, Virginia Nylander, *Niñez: Spanish Songs, Games, and Stories of Childhood* (Santa Fe, Sunstone Press, 1993)

Ebinger, Virginia Nylander, *De Colores* (New York, Schott, 1992)

*Ellis, Karen, *Domino: Traditional Children's Songs, Proverbs, and Culture from the American Virgin Islands* (Narbeth PA, Guavaberry, 1990)

Fowke, Edith, *Sally Go Round the Sun* (Canada, McClelland and Stewart, 1981)

François, Raymond, *Yé Yaille, Chère! Traditional Cajun Dance Music* (Lafayette LA, Thunderstone Press, 1990)

*Fukuda, Hanako, *Favorite Songs of Japanese Children* (Van Nuys, Alfred, 1964, 1990)

Fulton, Eleanor and Pat Smith, *Let's Slice the Ice* (St. Louis, Magnamusic-Baton, 1978)

Fuoco-Lawson, G., *Street Games* (London, Schott, 1989)

Gomme, Alice B. *The Traditional Games of England, Scotland and Ireland* (London, Thames and Hudson Ltd, 1984)

*Jones, Bessie and Bess Lomax Hawes, *Step It Down: Games, Plays, Songs & Stories from the Afro-American Heritage* (Athens GA, University of Georgia Press, 1972, 1987)

Knapp, M. and H., *One Potato, Two Potato* (New York, W.W. Norton & Company, 1976)

***Langstaff, Nancy and John,** *Sally Go Round the Moon: And other Revels Songs and Singing Games for Young Children* (Cambridge MA, Revels Publications, 1986)

Meek, Bill, *Moon Penny: Irish Children's Songs, Rhymes and Tongue-twisters* (Dublin, Ossia)

Newell, William Wells, *Games and Songs of American Children* (New York, Dover Press, 1963)

***Nguyen, Phong and Patricia Shehan Campbell,** *From Rice Paddies and Temple Yards: Traditional Music of Vietnam* (Danbury CT, World Music Press, 1990)

Opie, Iona and Peter, *Children's Games in Street and Playground* (New York and Oxford, Oxford University Press, 1985)

Opie, Iona and Peter, *The Singing Game* (New York and Oxford, Oxford University Press, 1985)

***Orozco, Jose-Luis,** *Lirica Infantil: Cancionero, Children's Folklore in Spanish* (Berkeley, Arcoiris, 1991)

***Punana Leo Cultural Centers,** *Pai Ka Leo: A Collection of Original Hawaiian Songs for Children* (Honolulu, Bess Press, 1989)

Rohrbough, Lynn, revised by Cecilia Riddell, *Handy Play Party Book* (Burnsville NC, World Around Songs, 1982)

Rubin, Rose N. and Michael Stillman, eds., *A Russian Song Book* (New York, Dover, 1989)

***Sam, Sam-Ang and Patricia Shehan Campbell,** *Silent Temples, Songful Hearts: Traditional Music of Cambodia* (Danbury CT, World Music Press, 1991)

Savoy, Ann Allen, *Cajun Music: A Reflection of a People* (Eunice, LA, 1984)

***Seeger, Ruth Crawford,** *American Folk Songs for Children* (New York, Doubleday, 1975)

***Serwadda, W. Moses,** *Songs and Stories from Uganda* (Danbury CT, World Music Press, 1974)

Shiu-Ying, Fung, *Chinese Children's Games* (New York, A.R.T.S. Inc., 1983)

***Steinberg, Judith and Victor Cockburn, Eds.,** *Where I Come From! 63 Songs and Poems from Many Cultures* (Boston, Talking Stone Productions, 1991)

Tempest, Peter, *Nesting Doll Rhymes* (Chicago, Imported Publications, for Malysh Publishers, 320 West Ohio St, Chicago, IL 60610)

Chinese - *Péng yǒu*
English - *Friends*
French - *Amis*
Gaelic - *Cáirde*
Hebrew - *Chaverim*
Japanese - *Tomodachi*
Spanish - *Amigos*

What other languages can you say "Friends" in?

Facts and Figures

Asia

Country	Area (sq. miles)	Population	Language	Capital	Products	Religion
Cambodia	70,000	6,200,000	Khmer	Phnom Penh	Rice, Rubber	Theravada Buddhist
China	3,705,390	1,140,000,000	Cantonese Mandarin, local dialects	Beijing	Textiles, Industrial & Agricultural	Buddhist, Taoist, Muslim, Christian
India	1,269,340	844,000,000	Hindi, English, local dialects	New Delhi	Tea, Industrial, Jute, Textiles	Hindu, Muslim, Christian, Sikh, Buddhist, Jain
Japan	145,834	123,500,000	Japanese	Tokyo	Optical Equipment, Ships, Vehicles, Machinery, Electronic Goods, Chemicals, textiles	Shinto, Buddhist
South Korea	38,025	42,000,000	Korean	Seoul	Textiles, manufactured goods, chemicals	Buddhist, Christian, Chondokyoist
Malaysia	127,326	15,700,000	Malay	Kuala Lumpur	Rubber, tin, petroleum prod. palm oil, timber	Muslim
Vietnam	128,401	66,000,000	Vietnamese	Hanoi	Fish, coal, agricultural goods	Buddhist

ᔓFacts and Figures

Africa

Country	Area (sq. miles)	Population	Language	Capital	Products	Religion
Eritrea	36, 170	3,200,000	Tighriyna, Tigre, Arabic, Amharic	Asmara	Cotton, coffee, tobacco	Christian, Muslim
Mozambique	302,352	13,900,000	Portugese, Ronga, Shangana, Tswa, Tsonga	Maputo	Cashews, sugar, vegetables, fruit,	Various tribal traditional, Muslim, Catholic

ᔓFacts and Figures

Middle East

Country	Area (sq. miles)	Population	Language	Capital	Products	Religion
Iran	636,343	45,100,000	Persian, Farsi	Tehran	Oil, natural gas, cotton	Muslim
Israel	8,020	4,200,000	Hebrew, Arabic English, Yiddish	Jerusalem	Cut diamonds, chemicals, fruit, tobacco	Jewish, Muslim, Christian

Facts and Figures

Europe

Country	Area (sq. miles)	Population	Language	Capital	Products	Religion
England	50,333	46,000,000	English	London	Manufactured goods, electrical and engineering products, transport equipment, textiles, chemicals, plastics	Protestant
France	211,223	55,000,000	French	Paris	Cars, electrical equipment, wine, cereals, textiles, leather goods, chemicals, iron, steel	Roman Catholic
Ireland	27,138	3,600,000	English, Gaelic	Dublin	Meat and meat products, dairy products, beer, whiskey	Roman Catholic
Russia	8,650,166 combined	278,000,000 combined	Russian	Moscow	Iron, steel, chemicals, timber, paper, textiles, food, consumer goods	Russian Orthodox

Facts and Figures

North America and Caribbean

Culture	Area (sq. miles)	Population	Language	Capital	Products	Religion
Cajun	"Cajun triangle" approx. 10,000	1,000,000	Cajun French English	Mamou, Eunice, Lafayette, LA	Accordions, rice, alligators, crawfish soybeans, culinary	Catholic
Comanche	N/A	4,718	English	Lawton OK Anadarko OK Ft. Sill OK	Cattle ranching	Protestant, Native American Church
Georgia Sea Islands	3,644	386,415	English, Gullah	N/A	Corn, potatoes, oysters, shrimp, diversified farming	Christian
Navajo	160,000	260,000	Navajo, English	Window Rock, AZ	Timber, textiles, minerals, Navajo educational materials, tourism	Peyote, Christian, Traditional
New Mexico	121,593	1,581,227	English, Spanish	Santa Fe	Lumber, minerals, printing, foods, transportation	
Puerto Rico	3,492	3,580,332	Spanish, English	San Juan	Coffee, fruit, sugar, pharmaceuticals, petroleum refining, tourism	Roman Catholic

Facts and Figures

South America

Country	Area (sq. miles)	Population	Language	Capital	Products	Religion
Brazil	3,286,727	138,400,000	Portuguese	Brasilia	Machinery, vehicles, soya beans, coffee, cocoa	Christian
Ecuador	109,491	8,900,000	Spanish, Quechua	Quito	Oil, textiles, bananas, cocoa, coffee, rice	Roman Catholic

Index

Book/audio sets from World Music Press...

You will enjoy all our award-winning, in-depth yet accessible book-and-recording sets of music from around the world. Most take a long look at one culture in particular, include lots of photos, musical transcriptions, cultural background information and a companion recording of every song or piece included in the book. The companion recordings feature performances by musicians from the highlighted tradition in almost all cases. All are appropriate for use with all grade levels and Introduction to World Music or college music education courses, home study use and community outreach programs and library collections--or simply if you love music.

All Hands On! An Introduction to West African Percussion Ensembles
Lynne Jessup (Book or Book/CD set)

A Singing Wind: Songs and Melodies from Ecuador
Elizabeth Villarreal Brennan (Book/CD set)

Flowing Waters: Building a Musical Bridge Between Your Orff-Schulwerk Ensemble and the Javanese Gamelan
Lillian Holtfreter with FX Widaryanto (Video/Manual)

From Rice Paddies and Temple Yards: Traditional Music of Vietnam
Phong Nguyen and Patricia Shehan Campbell (American Folklife Center Award) (Book/CD)

Hot Marimba! Zimbabwean-Style Music for Orff Instruments
Walt Hampton (Book/CD)

La-Li-Luo Dance Songs of the Chuxiong Yi, Yunnan Province, China
Alan Thrasher (Not appropriate for the lower grades.) (Book or Book/Cass.)

Let Your Voice Be Heard! Songs from Ghana and Zimbabwe (Tenth Anniversary Edition)
Abraham Kobena Adzenyah, Dumisani Maraire, Judith Cook Tucker (Book/CD)

The Lion's Roar! Chinese Luogu Percussion Ensembles
Han Kuo-huang, Patricia Shehan Campbell (Book/CD.; optional set of 13 slides)

Los Mariachis! An Introduction to the Mariachi Tradition of Mexico
Patricia Harpole and Mark Fogelquist (director of El Mariachi Uclatlan) (Book/CD)

Marimba Mojo! More Zimbabwean-Style Music for Orff Instruments
Walt Hampton (Book/cass. or Book/CD)

More Pandemonium! Three Caribbean Pieces for Orff Ensembles
Deborah Teason (Book/cassette)

Moving Within the Circle: Contemporary Native American Music and Dance
Bryan Burton (Book/CD; 20 color slides also available with teacher's guide)

My Harvest Home: A Celebration of Polish Songs, Dances and Customs
Andrea Schafer; illustrated by Peter Schafer (Book/CD)

Pandemonium Rules! Orff Instrument Arrangements of Steel Band Ensembles
Deborah Teason and Gage Averill with Pandemonium Steel Band (Book/Cass.)

Roots & Branches: A Legacy of Multicultural Music for Children
Patricia Shehan Campbell, Ellen McCullough-Brabson, Judith Cook Tucker (Book/CD)

Saman: Dance of a Thousand Hands
I Gusti Ngurah Kertayuda and Bob Walser (Video/Teacher's Manual)

Silent Temples, Songful Hearts: Traditional Music of Cambodia
Sam-Ang Sam and Patricia Shehan Campbell (American Folklife Center Award) (Book/CD)

Sing and Shine On! An Innovative Guide to Leading Multicultural Song
Nick Page

Songs and Stories from Uganda
Moses Serwadda, illustrated by Leo and Diane Dillon (Book/CD)

Voices of the Wind: Native American Flute Songs
Bryan Burton, with Maria Pondish Kreiter (Book/CD or Book/cass.)

Welcome in the Spring: Morris and Sword Dances for Children
Paul Kerlee (Book+1CD of morris musicians; Book+2CDs—morris musicians plus Orff inst. demo)

Welcome to Mussomeli: Children's Songs from an Italian Country Town
Rosella Diliberto (with Bryan Burton) (Book/CD)

When the Earth Was Like New: Western Apache Songs and Stories
Chesley Goseyun Wilson, Ruth Wilson, Bryan Burton (Book/CD)

World Music Press — Visit our website for full descriptions: www.worldmusicpress.com